ROI

Practical Theory and Innovative Applications

ROI

Practical Theory and Innovative Applications

Robert A. Peters

A Division of American Management Associations

Library of Congress Cataloging in Publication Data

Peters, Robert A
   ROI; practical theory and innovative applications.

   1. Capital investments. 2. Cash flow. 3. Profit--
Accounting. I. Title.
HG4028.C4P38   332.6'34   73-93043
ISBN 0-8144-5360-0

© 1974 AMACOM
A division of American Management Associations, New York.
All rights reserved. Printed in the United States of America.

First printing

Preface

THE "income and expense statement," which attempts to match costs against revenues, has been the traditional measure of financial accomplishment. In recent decades, however, two evolutionary changes in the environment of business have eroded its value. First, a combination of technical and social advances has increasingly substituted capital for labor in manufacturing. Second, profit itself as normally reported has become a product of many artificial and transient influences such as depreciation practices, tax laws, and latitude in "generally accepted accounting principles." Consequently, a genuine need exists to devise a better standard for measuring financial results. The increasing dominance of capital, or cash, in terms of both an investment and a return suggests that these outflows and inflows can provide a more incisive basis for metering business progress.

Of even greater importance, statistics also show that since World War II the sharp rise in capital employed by durable goods manufacturers has produced an ever deteriorating reward. While dollar earnings have continued in an upward trend, the investment necessary to generate these earnings has risen faster; consequently, return on investment has been declining steadily. American industry is being threatened with economic malnutrition. The danger signals are clear, and a need for understanding and attention to this matter has become vital. One is reminded that interest in the subjects of pollution and the energy crisis also was lagging for many years, even though evidence was available to identify increasing cause for concern.

Though "return on investment" is both familiar and generally accepted as a concept, suitable mechanics for applying it comprehensively have been lacking. Only for individual investment decisions has ROI begun to come into common use. In this book, the author offers a cash-oriented ROI approach to business economics that is theoretically sound, easy to understand and employ, and virtually universal in its applicability. Discussion begins with a documentation of the alarming trend toward more investment, less return. Then the problems associated with traditional concepts of profit are identified. After the reader is warned against a number of inaccurate simulations of ROI, a fundamental theory from which all true applications may flow is offered—a technique as uncomplicated and utilitarian as the safety pin. Next is an explanation of how this basic approach is adapted for a total business. Succeeding chapters describe essentially new or seldom employed ways to provide ROI insight and analysis of business results. Finally, Chapter 11 shows how ROI dominates and governs earnings-per-share trends, and warns that indefinite continuation of improvement in EPS is impossible unless the widespread decline in ROI is arrested.

The book is addressed to general management and financial executives. It is intended to be easy to read, practical, and nontechnical. It is brief and to the point—a primer rather than a dissertation. The orientation is primarily toward a manufacturing business in contrast to one emphasizing service, distribution, financing, or advanced technology. But the principles are applicable anywhere; only the examples need be revised. Because the subject matter is so broad and far-reaching, not all questions are answered or every detail refined. Instead, the purpose of this book may be summarized in the adage: It is better to light a candle than to curse the darkness.

The assistance of Mr. R. T. Waring is acknowledged with thanks. Mr. Waring put together several of the illustrations, proofread the manuscript, and also argued theory with me from time to time.

Robert A. Peters

Contents

1

Sounding
the Alarm

A BUSINESSMAN is scanning the morning newspaper. An article announces that the price of jute imported from India will soar because of a severe drought out in the provinces. The reader's mind idles along in neutral; he is in auto parts, and could care less what happens to jute in India. A primary function of management is to separate the important from the casually interesting. Time is a precious resource; it cannot be wasted on irrelevant matters.

The subject of this book is not only important—it is vital. It would be one thing if a discussion about profits, cash flow, investment, and the like were only an academic debate among accountants searching for an additional modicum of precision. But it's much more than that. American industry, collectively, is in trouble, and trends are continuing to go in the wrong direction. This is not an idle cry of alarm to attract attention. It is very real, and very frightening. The rewards of business have been declining in relation to the investment required to produce those rewards. We are fast approaching the critical point where prospective rewards will not justify the perpetuation of "free enterprise" as we know it today.

Chart 1-1 shows that over the past 25 years not only have profits declined in relationship to the equity of shareholders but, much more important, the return on investment earned by durable goods manufacturers has fallen even more and now can only be classified as marginal.

The "return on investment" shown in Chart 1-1 is calculated according to the technique described in Chapter 5 of this book; it is a very real number, directly comparable with the familiar interest rate on savings accounts, bonds, and so on. But almost any way

CHART 1-1. Profit/equity and return on investment for U.S. manufacturers of durable goods, 1947-1972.

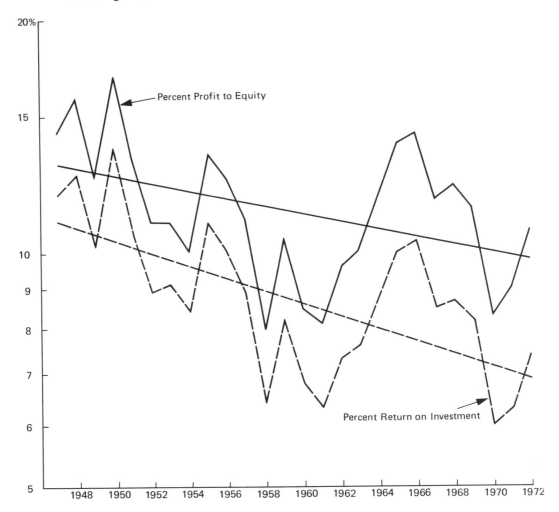

SOURCE: Calculated from raw data in the Federal Trade Commission's *Quarterly Financial Report.*

one puts together data involving profit or cash flow on one side, and some definition of investment on the other, the trend lines point the same way—down! These are, of course, averages; some companies have done better, others not as well. But collectively the industrial bastion of our economic system is being seriously undermined. The statistics on which this and other charts in Chapter 1 are based, together with additional related information, are contained in Appendix A.

In the late 1940s, business depreciated its assets over an average life of about 20 years. In recent years, however, book depreciation rates for manufacturers of durable goods now average closer to 15 years. The significance of this is very great. Economic obsolescence as a result of advancing technology has a much greater impact than it used to. And the trend undoubtedly will continue, since the rate of technological progress shows no sign of leveling off. While cash flows are being stimulated by the increased depreciation, the need to modernize also is demanding reinvestment more quickly than before. Even with the stimulus given to cash flow by depreciation, total cash flow (profit and depreciation) in relation to investment has declined. As a consequence, business has been forced to take on additional debt. Much of this debt has been justified under the banner of expansion, but unfortunately it has in reality resulted from industry's inability to earn enough of a return to provide the capital needed to maintain itself in a viable state. Chart 1-2 tells the story.

From the vantage point of shareholders, cash flow in relation to equity actually has improved slightly, and acted as a tranquilizer or mask to the aforementioned danger signals (Chart 1-3). But this is a phony. The "improvement" is exclusively the result of a sharp increase in the percentage of debt as a part of capitalization, as shown in Chart 1-4. The real problem therefore has been obscured. Chart 1-5, using hypothetical numbers for an illustration, shows how this phenomenon can and did happen.

CHART 1-2. Cash flow/investment and annual depreciation rate for U.S. manufacturers of durable goods, 1947-1972.

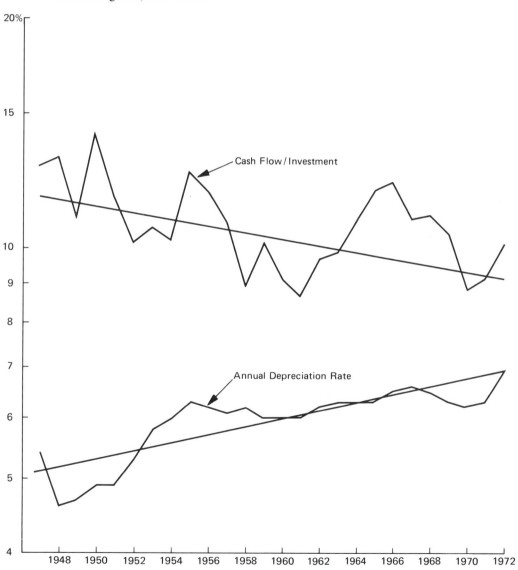

SOURCE: Calculated from raw data in the Federal Trade Commission's *Quarterly Financial Report.*

CHART 1-3. Cash flow/equity for U.S. manufacturers of durable goods, 1947–1972.

CHART 1-4. Debt/capitalization for U.S. manufacturers of durable goods, 1947–1972.

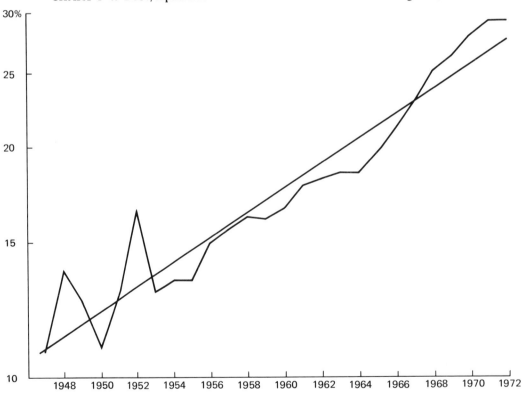

SOURCE: Both charts were calculated from raw data in the Federal Trade Commission's *Quarterly Financial Report.*

4

CHART 1-5. Hypothetical example of ostensible improvement in cash flow/equity ratio with simultaneous decline in other measures of performance.

	Decade 1	Decade 2	Decade 3
	Ratio: 10–90[a]	Ratio: 20–80[a]	Ratio: 30–70[a]
Debt	$ 10	$ 40	$ 90
Equity	90	160	210
Investment	100	200	300
Profit	15	20	25
Depreciation	10	25	37
Cash Flow	25	45	62
Measures of performance (calculated from above data):			
Cash flow/equity	27.8%	28.1%	29.5%
Cash flow/investment	25.0	22.5	20.7
Profit/equity	16.7	12.5	11.9
Profit/investment	15.0	10.0	8.3

[a] Debt and equity percentages of total investment.

If all this isn't enough, the persistent inflation of recent years has further aggravated matters. Today's profits and cash flows are being measured against yesterday's cost of assets, which of itself tends to produce an illusion of well-being that is totally unwarranted. These subjects are discussed in more depth later.

In a few words: Business desperately needs new tools, for the old ones are leading us down the primrose path. When returns become insufficient to attract capital, economic stagnation and decay are inevitable. There isn't much time left to change direction.

2

Problems with Profit as a Measure of Accomplishment

MOST of the discussion in this book focuses on the "how to" of return on investment. However, there is no point in reading about proposed solutions without an understanding of the problem itself. The first two chapters tell *why* businessmen need to be concerned with the topic.

The "problem" addressed in this chapter is profit, and the fact that it no longer means what most people think it means, or what it used to mean, or in all probability what it will mean in the future. Sometimes the mental image of a word or phrase becomes so strong that it blocks out any notion that its definition may have changed, especially when the rate of change is so gradual as to be almost imperceptible. These are strong words, and deliberately so. It is worth repeating that a recognition of the problem must precede any solution, and that is the objective of this chapter.

Let's use the word "reward" in place of profit or return or whatever, and first emphasize that this book fully supports the concept of such a reward in relation to an input—no matter what words are used. The term "profit," however, brings to mind a specific percentage or amount at the bottom of a profit and loss statement—a form of reward. This form, this report, this definition still is useful. It just isn't as useful as it used to be—because it doesn't convey what it used to convey. And it's becoming progressively less meaningful as time passes. That is why a new measure of reward is necessary.

The diminishing utility of "profit" as discussed here has nothing to do with various well-publicized accounting machinations—purchasing and pooling of interest mergers, capitalization of costs formerly defined customarily as expenses, reductions in pension-fund contributions because of more optimistic actuarial or appreciation estimates, and so on. These are important subjects, but they are not the theme of this book. It will be assumed that bottom-line results as shown were calculated in a generally acceptable manner. The issue is the intrinsic value of the profit number itself.

This chapter will discuss the circumstances and events that have eroded the value of "profit" as a measure of accomplishment. But first, one more caveat should be mentioned.

The book title and these few words of introduction may have stimulated some readers to look forward to the unveiling of a magic new formula or technique that will not only supplant current reporting and evaluation methods but will, of itself, present a universal financial panacea under any and all conditions. Conceptually, perhaps so. Practically speaking, however, there is no such thing. The attempt here is to identify the need for improvement, and to suggest and define a philosophy that can assist business-men in achieving a proper monetary reward. No cure-all is offered.

The Problem of Relating Profit to Sales

So what's wrong with profit in its traditional percentage relationship to sales? First, and most important, the hose is attached to the wrong faucet. It isn't the flow of funds beginning with sales income and cost-of-goods-sold outgo that is primary; rather, the issue is how much was invested in the business in relation to the reward generated by that investment.

If you study an annual report of a firm in the grocery business, for example, you will more than likely find that for years they have been earning about 1% or 2% net on sales, and yet in the text of the report seem to be contented with these results. On the other hand, the annual report of a heavy-industry concern might show a profit of as much as 10%, but the text will indicate they are not completely satisfied. How can this be? If percentages mean anything, why isn't everyone in heavy industry and not in the grocery business? The obvious answer must be that a measuring stick of percent profit to sales is not of itself an incisive way to make comparisons among different industries. But when assets employed are recognized (irrespective at this point of how assets are defined), the resulting equation provides common ground for comparisons. A combination of sales, profits, and assets into a loosely defined type of return on investment is shown in Chart 2-1. The formula is not the one advocated in this book, but it serves as a useful intro-duction to the topic.

By canceling out "sales" in the two parts of the equation, the relationship of profit to assets remains and, very simply, is one of the common definitions of "return on in-vestment." In this particular expression, the reference is to reported profits rather than

CHART 2-1. Formula for a rudimentary form of return on investment.

$\dfrac{\text{Profit}}{\text{Sales}}$	$\times$	$\dfrac{\text{sales}}{\text{assets}}$	$=$	% return
% profit	$\times$	asset turnover	$=$	% return

cash flow or something else in order to provide a link with the profit-to-sales ratio. Although one may cancel out the sales factor in both parts of the equation and show only the ratio of profit to investment, it is better to leave these two components intact, because each of them has a story to tell.

Look again at the grocery store and the heavy-industry concern. Their respective returns on investment (in this definition of the term) might be equal in spite of the wide difference in profit margins. Chart 2-2 shows how. One can see that the grocery store recorded a very low percentage profit on each item sold, but didn't have much in the way of assets invested in the business, so annual sales were ten times the amount of assets. Thus, only a very small profit margin was needed to produce a high return on investment. On the other hand, heavy industry is characterized by an extremely high asset base, to the point that annual sales in this illustration just matched the amount of the investment. So a high profit margin on sales was required to record a good return.

The above illustrations are not academic; they are only somewhat extreme for emphasis. Over a period of time, profit margins should and do vary with capital intensity, assuming comparable business risks. They always have, and they always will. "Five percent after tax" may be great for some companies, but totally unsatisfactory for others. Even within an industry, or a single company, profit margins may properly vary if there are significant differences in capital intensity. This is a fact. Pause and reflect on it.

The terms "asset turnover" and "percent return" in Charts 2-1 and 2-2 imply an annual basis. In other words, asset turnover is the division of annual sales by the assets employed during the period. When only one month is considered, all of the assets are in use but sales are only about one-twelfth of the total for the year. Thus the sales must be annualized before making a calculation. This shouldn't be hard to understand, because in reference to, say, 5% interest, one normally thinks of it as an annual rate.

This characteristic of profit margins varying with capital intensity is one that politicians, among others, often find convenient. Particularly in an election year, votes can be gained by excoriating corporations with "fat profit margins"—generally those requiring a heavy investment in order to conduct their business. On the other side of the fence, companies characterized by a high asset turnover and therefore small profit margins often "poor mouth" their fortunes—partly, no doubt, to ward off any who might accuse them of becoming rich. For example, following is a brief quotation from an annual report of a

CHART 2-2. Formula and example of a rudimentary form of return on investment.

$\dfrac{\text{Profit}}{\text{Sales}}$	$\times$	$\dfrac{\text{sales}}{\text{assets}}$	$=$	% return
% profit	$\times$	asset turnover	$=$	% return
Grocery store:		$\dfrac{1}{100} \times \dfrac{100}{10}$	$=$	10%
Heavy industry:		$\dfrac{10}{100} \times \dfrac{100}{100}$	$=$	10%

well-known company in the latter group. The chairman and president are addressing the stockholders:

> In a recent study a representative group of Americans were asked to give their opinions as to what percentage of each dollar of sales they thought the average business made in profit after the payment of expenses and taxes. The median estimate was 27%. . . .
>
> Obviously, many people just don't seem to know, because the actual figure is 5.1%. For your company it was only 3.1%. In other words, profit is approximately 5¢ out of every dollar of sales for U.S. industry as a whole and approximately 3¢ for your company.

(By the way, this same company's ROI, calculated in a manner described later in the book, was considerably above average!)

To repeat, just because one business earns 4% after tax and another makes 8% doesn't of itself signify the latter is better. It is imperative that in one form or another recognition be given to the investment required to achieve these profits. If management does not pay attention to this fact of life voluntarily, ultimately they must do so under duress. Far too many executives fall into the trap of placing primary stress on the profit dollar without adequate consideration of how much horsepower or money-power it takes to generate these profits.

On a smaller scale this scenario is repeated regularly. A new nightclub opens up; the building is superbly designed and engineered, furnishings are the finest, landscaping and grounds are lavish–and a year later the place is in receivership. The padlock on the door is not always related to the quality of food or service, or to the absence of sexy entertainment; often, there was just too much money tied up to make any kind of return. After the club goes through bankruptcy a time or two, the cost base finally is lowered to the point where the same sales and profit dollars may provide an acceptable return to a prudent investor.

The problem just discussed centers on the *relationship* of profit to sales, not the composition or integrity of the profit dollar. That comes next.

The Problem
of Accounting
for Depreciation

Another important difficulty with reported profit as a measure of performance relates directly to the investment. Conventional accounting practice dictates that costs of facilities and equipment whose useful lives exceed one year be capitalized–that is, recorded as an investment or asset–rather than be expensed or entirely charged against profits in the year the outlays took place. Then, their costs or basic values are distributed over the useful asset lives in a systematic manner. This is the familiar concept of depreciation. Similar treatment is applicable for depletion of wasting resources and amortization of intangible costs. Any good accounting text will provide amplification of this theory which, though simple in essence, has provoked much controversy in practice.

Here we shall be concerned primarily with the connection between depreciation and profit. Depreciation is linked to both investment and reported profit and, in addition, introduces another dimension usually called "cash flow." To say it another way, reported profits are influenced by charges for a share of depreciation expense, and the amount of such charges is in turn influenced by the capital investment. But though depreciation charges reduce reported profits and the base on which tax payments are calculated, they do not of themselves involve any outlay of cash—the cash having been paid out when the capital facilities were first purchased. The point is that "profits" are not at all synonymous with "cash."

Now let's explore the significance of this. Look at Chart 2-3. Assume these two companies to be alike in every respect except in their attitude toward depreciation. Observe that Company A, which shows a higher reported profit, both in absolute dollars and as a percentage of sales, actually has a lower cash flow than Company B. The difference is caused entirely by the fact that Company A, having recorded a higher profit, is obliged to pay more in taxes. Writing a check to the government reduces cash, and that's all there is to it.

But wait a minute. How can this be? Where did the difference in depreciation come from if the hypothesis stated that the companies were alike in every other respect? The answer is that depreciation has become a matter of judgment. True, there are rules, but managements are permitted considerable latitude within the broad framework of government and accounting regulations.

It was stated earlier that the concept of depreciation merely involves spreading the cost of an asset over its useful life rather than "expensing" it all at once. These two companies have identical machines which cost $180. Mr. A says the machine is good for nine years, so he takes one-ninth of the cost ($20) against the current year. Mr. B says the machine will last six years, and therefore takes one-sixth, or $30, of the cost against the current year. It's as simple as that. Will the machines actually last nine and six years respectively? Maybe so and maybe not. If not, adjustments to depreciation will have to be made later, and in an ongoing enterprise, "later" can be the indefinite future. The point is that a profit and loss statement, or a cash flow statement, is not concerned about "later"—it is concerned about "now." It is this year's profit or cash flow everyone is tracking on; tomorrow is another subject.

CHART 2-3. Relationship of depreciation to profit and cash flow.

	Company A	Company B
Sales	$100	$100
Various expenses (excluding depreciation)	60	60
Depreciation	20	30
Profit before tax	20	10
Tax	10	5
Profit after tax	10	5
Cash reconciliation:		
Income from sales	100	100
Various expenses	60	60
Taxes	10	5
Cash left over	30	35
Profit reported on books	10	5
Plus depreciation	20	30
Equals cash on hand	30	35

The condition portrayed in Chart 2-3 may have stemmed from another cause. Perhaps Company B assumed the same total useful life for the asset as Company A—nine years—but chose to adopt an accelerated method of depreciation which charged to expense a greater share of the cost in the early years of the asset's life. All perfectly legal and within the framework of "generally accepted accounting principles." Obviously, Company B will be obliged to charge less depreciation (and pay more taxes) in later years, since only the total amount of the purchase can be depreciated—but again, tomorrow is another subject. Chart 2-3 also could apply to two companies that use the same assumption of asset life and have adopted the same practices for accelerated depreciation, but the asset purchased by Company B is newer and therefore in an earlier phase of the charge pattern under an accelerated method.

If the same total depreciation is eventually charged by both, and their tax bills ultimately will be even, why all the furor? Well, business is an ongoing thing. Companies are buying new assets year after year. Thus, a consistent application of either of these approaches perpetuates the situation portrayed in Chart 2-3, and only when growth stops and spending is reduced will the tide reverse. Until that time, one might say that accelerated depreciation provides a permanent cash advance from Uncle Sam by reason of not having to pay till some indefinite future date the taxes another fellow is paying now. And, as we shall see later, cash now is always a plus, because even when placed in a savings account, money will increase its value year by year. Furthermore, maybe someday in the future the owner of Company B will sell out the business and be able to get a nice capital gain, which is taxed at a lower rate, and thereby convert a temporary advantage into a permanent one.

"Book" Versus "Tax" Depreciation

The cash-versus-profit issue is further complicated when book and tax treatments of depreciation are different, a condition completely acceptable—even becoming customary—under today's "generally accepted accounting principles." In other words, one number representing depreciation is reported to the shareholders, but another (larger) number is used when calculating the profit base on which taxes are paid.

Back in the '50s, when accelerated depreciation was first allowed as a deduction for tax purposes, most companies took advantage of the tax saving and automatically included the same figures in their annual reports. But during the '60s, pressures for improvement in earnings became irresistible, and led to the current practice of reporting lower, straight-line depreciation (and higher earnings) to the public while at the same time showing higher depreciation (and lower taxable earnings) to the government. The justification usually went something like this: "Let's take advantage of all the tax breaks, but we really believe straight-line depreciation to better reflect proper accounting." After one corporate member of an industry adopted this dual standard, others felt obliged to follow in order to avoid unfavorable comparisons. Thus, industry after industry made the switch. Now comparatively few still hold to a single reporting method for all purposes.

Chart 2-4 shows how it works. Note that a company taking less depreciation for book purposes than for tax shows higher reported earnings, but not to the full extent of the pretax difference. The usual reasoning is that someday a tax must be paid on the extra pretax income reported, and if it's considered proper to report the income for book purposes, one ought to at least show against it the tax that someday will be due.

CHART 2-4. Difference in reported results of book and tax depreciation.

	Statistics Reported to Shareholders	Statistics Used for Tax Purposes
Pretax income before depreciation	$800	$800
Depreciation	100	200
Pretax income	700	600
Federal income tax @ 50%:		
Current (paid in this period)	300	300
Deferred (accrued for future payment)	50	—
Total taxes	350	300
Net income	350	300
Cash flow:		
Net income	350	300
Depreciation	100	200
Deferred taxes (tax effect of accelerated method)	50	—
Total cash flow	500	500

Because the due date is postponed—some say forever—the obligation is classified as a deferred rather than a current tax liability.

Here's where we are on the matter of depreciation. There are two sets of rules—one involving "generally accepted accounting principles" which must be followed in order to qualify for an auditor's certification, and tax regulations which dictate what can and cannot be done in establishing the profit base for a tax calculation. Within each set a certain amount of latitude is allowed so long as there is consistency in application of the practice selected.

The traumatic aspect of the depreciation problem is that methods which tend to "improve" reported profits may have the opposite effect on cash flow. In a small company or proprietorship without a lot of shareholders to keep happy or the investment community to worry about, most businessmen will try to write off as much as they can as fast as they can. There's little worry about what others might think—all they want is the money. But in large companies there is much pressure for reported earnings, because this is the way so many people evaluate results. As noted previously, the solution to this dilemma adopted by many, if not most, large companies is to report one calculation of profit to the government and another to the shareholders, as shown in Chart 2-4. Stop and think for a minute. How much profit do *you* think the company really made?

This discussion has concentrated on depreciation, but a parallel situation exists in other noncash "expenses" such as amortization of goodwill, patents, and capitalized research costs. In recent years these types of noncash charges have had an ever greater influence on reported profits, both because of their more common occurrence and as a result of liberalization of accepted methods of accounting for them in P&L statements.

This book will not attempt to pursue further the issues just reviewed. In all probability, professional accountants and regulatory bodies will be wrestling with them for a long time yet—and management cannot wait. Instead, we shall address ourselves to another approach which is much more tangible and infinitely more useful.

Look again at Chart 2-4. Notice that regardless of the method used for profit reporting, cash flow is the same—cash flow consisting of reported profit (whatever it may be), book depreciation, and the increase in deferred taxes. It also can be demonstrated that while different approaches to book depreciation may affect reported profit, they have no effect whatsoever on cash flow. Chart 2-5 uses the data shown in Chart 2-4 and adds another column of numbers which considers an increase in book depreciation. Reported profits go down, but cash flow is unchanged. To say it another way, in a given year more depreciation for book purposes doesn't help cash flow but does hurt reported profits. Conversely, more depreciation for tax purposes doesn't help reported earnings but does improve cash flow.

CHART 2-5. Effect of change in book depreciation with no change in tax depreciation.

	Statistics Reported to Shareholders	Statistics Used for Tax Purposes	Statistics Reported to Shareholders	Statistics Used for Tax Purposes
Pretax income before depreciation	$800	$800	$800	$800
Depreciation	100	200	150	200
Pretax income	700	600	650	600
Federal income tax @ 50%:				
Current (paid in this period)	300	300	300	300
Deferred (accrued for future payment)	50	—	25	—
Total taxes	350	300	325	300
Net income	350	300	325	300
Cash flow:				
Net income	350	300	325	300
Depreciation	100	200	150	200
Deferred taxes (tax effect of accelerated method)	50	—	25	—
Total cash flow	500	500	500	500

In summary, the conclusion is that cash flow provides a better way to get a handle on results than does reported profit. If depreciation were only of nominal influence, this entire discussion would be a tempest in a teapot. But as business in general has become much more capital-intensive, depreciation correspondingly has grown to a very large number. In heavy industry, it is quite common for book depreciation to equal or exceed reported profits.

CHART 2-6. Comparison of selected results of new and old facilities.

	New Facility	Old Facility
Gross assets	$10,000,000	$ 5,000,000
Annual sales	10,000,000	10,000,000
Profit after tax	200,000	400,000
% profit to sales	2%	4%
% profit to gross assets	2%	8%

New Facilities vs.
Old Facilities:
Pitfalls
with Numbers

Quite often profit comparisons between companies comprised primarily of new facilities and those with older assets can be misleading. Management may continue to devote energies to an older plant or a product showing an acceptable profit-to-sales ratio, when in reality they ought to let it die and instead concentrate their efforts on better opportunities. Trouble is, the figures as usually reported don't provide any guidance.

Look at Chart 2-6. From the information presented, the old facility would seem to be ahead on three counts: higher absolute profit dollars, a better profit-to-sales ratio, and, if you want to say something about assets, a higher ratio of profit to gross (original-cost) assets. Not even a hint of a conflict, since all signs point in the same direction.

But review the same basic information with a little more detail (exaggerated for effect) in Chart 2-7. Now it might be a new ball game. The additional calculation of cash flow to assets shows a completely different picture. What now? Several things can be inferred. The old facility appears to be involved in the well-known practice of "milking the franchise"—taking out of the business as much as possible without putting in anything new; the very light depreciation rate suggests this. Such a practice is not automatically

CHART 2-7. Comparison of new and old facilities, considering additional information.

	New Facility	Old Facility
Gross assets	$10,000,000	$ 5,000,000
Annual sales	10,000,000	10,000,000
Profit before tax and before depreciation	1,400,000	900,000
Depreciation	1,000,000	100,000
Pretax profit	400,000	800,000
Tax	200,000	400,000
Profit after tax	200,000	400,000
% profit to sales	2%	4%
% profit to gross assets	2%	8%
Cash flow	1,200,000	500,000
% cash flow to gross assets	12%	10%

14

bad, especially if nothing new technologically has happened for years. There probably still is some machinery around to make buggy whips—not much, perhaps, but so long as a profitable market exists, why not?

Usually, however, it's the other way around. Our cities are full of old factories, large and small—antiquated buildings containing ancient equipment making obsolescent products, eking out an existence but no more. Loyal employees and the management have been at it for years and continue plodding along, seemingly oblivious to changes in products or processes in the world around them. Eventually there is a fire, or a death, or a government regulation—and the doors will close forever. It's only a matter of time.

The business that intends to perpetuate itself can't operate this way. Cash flows must be sufficient to provide for continuing modernization of equipment and technology. And financial acumen must be present to show the way. Conventional profit reporting does not raise a red flag when danger signs of this kind are developing, and management may be lulled into a false sense of security. But an analysis of cash flow and its relationship to the investment will highlight this issue. "Time to fix the roof is when the sun is shining."

Summary

In this chapter, three different types of illustrations were used to show why "profit" has been losing ground as the primary criterion of success. To recapitulate: (1) Under normal conditions, percent profit to sales varies widely according to the capital intensity of the industry being measured, because economic reality dictates that profit is more properly related to investment than to sales. (2) Varying depreciation and amortization practices can have a significant impact on reported profits, but a cash flow measure is not as greatly affected by bookkeeping techniques. (3) A cash-oriented indicator, when related to assets, provides management with incisive information about the economic viability of its facilities.

The balance of this book is an expansion of point 3.

3

What
Do You Mean
"ROI"?

CONCEPTUALLY, return on investment is not a new subject. One must ask, then: If the important needs just described are alleged to exist, why hasn't something been done by utilizing already existing return-on-investment techniques? Why hasn't a generally accepted accounting practice evolved by now?

No single reason seems to stand out. Undoubtedly the absence of dramatic incidents to attract attention and publicity to the matter has contributed to inertia. Also, a long-term trend of increase in the relative importance of capital has been obscured by normal business fluctuations; variations in depreciation practices have grown bit by bit over the past twenty years; and what some might call devices to manipulate reported profits have invaded industry on a gradual basis. Perhaps tradition and the accounting penchant for consistency have played a part, too.

But the greatest barrier to a generally accepted solution probably lies in the term "return on investment" itself. What do you mean "ROI"? Ask half a dozen different financial executives and it is likely that as many different answers will be forthcoming. ROI is truly the anomaly of the financial world. Although some aspects of accounting are conceded to involve more art than science, nowhere does the lack of universal definition, and the absence of uniformity in application, stand out so vividly as in the plethora of meanings and uses of the words "return on investment." Even though many will concede it to be the most important single measure of financial performance, there is little semblance of agreement in the industrial world on either how to define it or how to utilize it. It reminds one of the automobile industry right after World War I. Hundreds of companies were formed for the purpose of making gasoline-powered cars. Without intimate industry knowledge, a potential buyer at the time could only guess which car to purchase. But as time passed, only a few survived, and today the fingers of one hand are enough to record the domestic count. So return-on-investment applications will eventually become standardized—once a need for the "product" demands it.

Let's be specific and review some of the phraseology that marches under the banner of return on investment. Chart 3-1 is a partial listing of the options for measuring ROI. Next are two illustrations of the widely varying answers that can result from these different approaches. Chart 3-2 deals with an individual investment, while Chart 3-3 deals with a total business.

By now the problem should be coming into clearer focus. The great number of options stems from the fact that so many meanings can be applied to the word "return," to the word "investment," and to the implication of a time period associated with the phrase. The combinations are virtually infinite in number. Chart 3-4 pictures the situation.

A logical question at this point: Is one of these methods correct while the others are wrong? The answer to this two-part question is that one method stands out as being superior, but ROIs arrived at by alternative approaches also have some value as reference numbers when used consistently. Chapters 4 and 5 will identify the author's technique and justify the selection. As for the other methods, a focus of attention on investment, however defined, is better than nothing—and by a considerable margin. To some extent it also depends on the objective one is trying to accomplish. Obviously, shareholders will be interested in some kind of return on shareholders' equity; a return on replacement value of assets will be important to strategic planning; a business in which current assets are more important than fixed may choose to work with "profit" rather than "cash flow" because the difference in end result is small and problems involving depreciation are minimal; an industry which relies heavily on debt financing (credit companies and the like) may adapt an approach to fit its special needs. (Once again, the reader must avoid

CHART 3-1. Variety of ROI definitions and applications.

1.	Average annual profit ÷ average value of assets employed.
2.	Average annual cash flow ÷ average value of assets employed.
3.	Current-year profit ÷ gross assets.
4.	Current-year profit ÷ net assets.
5.	Current-year cash flow ÷ gross assets.
6.	Current-year cash flow ÷ net assets.
7.	Payback method (individual investment only).
8.–11.	Same as 3–6 above but substitute the words "shareholders' equity" for assets."
12.–15.	Same as 3–6 above but exclude the effect of interest on long-term debt (method of financing).
16.–19.	Same as 3–6 above but subtract current liabilities from assets.
20.+	Various combinations of 8–11 with 12–15 and 16–19, and combinations of 12–15 with 16–19.
Also:	A variety of discounted-cash-flow (present-value) applications. Modify any of the above to "capitalize" leaseholds. Adjust for goodwill or other intangible assets.

CHART 3-2. Varying results under different ROI techniques for evaluating individual investments.

	Year 1	Year 2	Year 3	Year 4	Year 5
Asset value–gross	$100	$100	$100	$100	$100
Less depreciation	20	40	60	80	100
Asset value–net	80	60	40	20	—
Profit generated by this asset	15	15	15	15	15
Cash flow (profit plus depreciation)	35	35	35	35	35

Some possible ROI measures:

Payback period = 6+ years on profit, 2+ years on cash.

Years 1 through 5: average annual profit as a % of gross assets	=	15%
Year 1: annual profit as a % of average beginning and ending net assets ($15 divided by $90)	=	16.7%
Year 4: annual profit as a % of average beginning and ending net assets ($15 divided by $30)	=	50%
Years 1 through 5: average annual profit as a % of average net assets ($15 divided by $50)	=	30%
Years 1 through 5: cash flow as a % of gross assets ($35 divided by $100)	=	35%
Year 1: cash flow as a % of average net assets ($35 divided by $90)	=	39%
Year 4: cash flow as a % of average net assets ($35 divided by $30)	=	117%

CHART 3-3. Varying results under different ROI techniques for evaluating a total business.

Current assets		$400	Current liabilities	$200
Fixed assets–gross	$500		Long-term debt (6%)	200
Less depreciation	200			
Net fixed assets		300	Equity	400
Goodwill		100		
Total assets		$800	Liabilities and capital	$800

Other statistics:	Profit	$ 80
	Depreciation	100
	Interest (pretax)	12

Some possible ROI measures:

Profit to net assets ($80 divided by $800)	=	10%
Profit to gross assets ($80 divided by $1,000)	=	8%
Profit to equity ($80 divided by $400)	=	20%
Cash flow to net assets ($180 divided by $800)	=	22.5%
Cash flow to gross assets ($180 divided by $1,000)	=	18%
Cash flow to equity ($180 divided by $400)	=	45%

Also: Same as above adjusted to exclude interest on long-term debt, or to exclude current liabilities, or to exclude goodwill, or to estimate fixed assets at replacement value.

CHART 3-4. Possible definitions of the term "return on investment."

RETURN	ON	INVESTMENT
annual	month	gross
average	year	net
profit	asset life	equity
cash		replacement
		adjusted

the trap of searching for a single financial measure that will, of itself, solve all his problems.)

But there is one *true* return on investment. A contradiction? No. Chapter 4 addresses that issue. The principal objective of this chapter has been to show that the confusing array of ROI terminology and the widely varying results of different approaches have discouraged many people from further pursuit of the matter. It's a jungle. Now let's thread a path through it.

4

ROI for an Individual Investment

IF you deposit $100 in a savings and loan association, there will be a sign on the premises saying "5% interest compounded quarterly" or "$4\frac{3}{4}$% interest with daily compounding," and even high school students know what it means. If you purchase a U.S. Government Series E savings bond for $75.00, five years later it will be worth $100.00, and the interest rate is 6%. If you buy a new home and assume a mortgage for $30,000 with equal monthly payments over 20 years of $251, the stated interest rate of 8% is an understandable number. If you are tardy in paying charge account obligations, the small print on the invoice may say that interest on the unpaid balance will be charged at the rate of $1\frac{1}{2}$% per month, or an 18% annual rate. A perusal of the financial columns in the daily newspaper will disclose quotations of the yield to maturity on various U.S. Treasury bonds and bills.

These are true returns on investment. Most everyone understands both the theory and the mechanics of the examples above. The commercial side of the business world works with these kinds of numbers every day. But the manufacturing side, for the most part, does not. Yet, virtually all individual business investment decisions can be expressed in a manner that will provide a result directly comparable to the above illustrations.

Think about it. No more mumbo jumbo that a certain investment in facilities produces, for example, an "average annual return on net assets" of X%. What do you mean "X%"? Is that good or bad? Your automobile is running rough, so it goes into the shop where the mechanic attaches some kind of scope and announces a reading of 24. Are his tones solemn? Or is there a smile on his face? That is the only way the uninitiated can infer whether a result of "24" indicates the trouble is major or minor. The same thing happens in manufacturing corporations. The chief accountant reports to the president that the company's proposed new plant is expected to show an ROI of $X\%$. A quick-thinking boss can only respond, "Is that up or down from the plant we built a few years ago?" and so limit his conclusion to the fact that this proposition is better or worse than the last one. What a pity. And so unnecessary.

To repeat, virtually all individual investment decisions can be evaluated in a manner that is directly comparable to interest on a savings bank deposit, or an E bond investment, or a home mortgage, or a yield on securities. If the true return on the new plant is, say, 6%, the president can (and perhaps should) retort: "Not good enough; we'd be better off putting our money into long-term bonds." If the answer is 40%, the president might well respond, "I don't believe you—look at the numbers again," because he knows from everyday life that such a high return on a complete new facility probably is unrealistic.

What an advantage to have a familiar reference point against which to evaluate investment decisions. Returns can be weighed against risks, and all sorts of judgments are made possible by additional calculations of alternative courses of action. Equally important, it's not necessary to add a staff of accountants to do it. The calculations themselves can be made amazingly simple.

Before continuing, a reminder that the ROI result projected under this—or any other—method will be only as valid as are the input assumptions on which the result is based. Thus, management understanding and approval of the basic data obviously are paramount. Books have been written on that subject alone.

Format for
the Calculation

If all business input/output decisions were as simple as those for savings accounts, E bonds, or straight-line mortgage payments, it is probable this approach would be well established by now in all corners of the business world. However, most investments are more complicated; inputs may be sequential, or results may vary year by year because of start-up expenses, accelerated depreciation, or whatever. So simple tables of amortization or compounding rates won't do the job. Instead, not only is a rather complex series of calculations necessary, but the iteration pattern itself must be tailor-made for each situation. It is not surprising, then, that most people have thrown up their hands because the mechanics are so formidable.

One person who didn't give up was a gentleman by the name of Ray I. Ruel—who, incidentally, was an industrial engineer, not an accountant. The July–August 1957 issue of *The Harvard Business Review* published his article titled "Profitability Index for Investments" (which still is worthwhile reading if you can find a copy). Some of the material in this chapter builds on Ruel's breakthrough contribution. The breakthrough was this: Ruel conceived a simple sequence or format which organized the investment requirements and the cash flows therefrom in a manner to facilitate the calculation of a true return on an investment—a practical way to put theory into practice.

Ruel called his method a "profitability index." Others using an essentially similar approach have titled it "discounted cash flow," "internal rate of return," "present value," or, as in this book, simply "return on investment." To the purist there may be differences, but for general managerial use the nuances associated with each of these titles are of little consequence. Lest academicians be offended, I hasten to add that research effort, with the objective of improving and purifying theory and practice, is as necessary and useful here as in other fields of endeavor. But business decisions cannot wait; we must do the best we can with what we have, using the "truth" as we know it.

For the next few pages, the objective will be to remove any mystery from the calculation form and build the reader's confidence that the technique is easy to use and that the resulting answer is a true ROI as he recognizes it from everyday life.

A simple one-page form containing the essentials is shown in Chart 4-1. There are three parts to it: the investment, the cash flow, and the calculation (ROI) section. First, the investment is posted on the form, segregating capital (depreciable) facilities, expensed items, and working funds for reasons that will become apparent as we go along. Next, annual after-tax profits, or savings, generated by the investment are recorded in the "Cash Flow" section. Depreciation also is detailed year by year, and added to profit to arrive at total cash flow. The column titled "Other" is used for investment credit, salvage value, return of working capital in the final year, and so on. Point zero is considered the moment of investment, and cash flows are recorded on an annual basis. (If month-by-month information were important the form could easily be adapted, but for most purposes annual results are sufficient.) Next, a series of calculations are made in the various "Trial" columns. The total annual cash flows are multiplied by the 5% discount factor for each year and posted in the 5% column; similarly for a 10% discount rate, and so on in succeeding columns. The present values in each of these columns then are added to obtain a total. The objective is to locate the discount rate which equates the present value of the future cash flows with the original investment, and that is the true return on investment. The interpolation section at the bottom facilitates "straight-lining" the difference between calculated rates, since it is unlikely a return will come out to exactly 5%, 10%, 15%, etc.

This is a "bare bones" format. The user may wish to flesh it out to include date, factory number, project number, approval signatures, and other supplementary data.

How to Use the
Calculation Form

For simplicity, we shall begin with only one investment and a single cash return. Later on, additional examples will be introduced to recognize sequential cash flows, both in constant and uneven amounts, and sequential investments.

This technique simply recognizes the time value of money. Would you rather have a dollar today or the promise of a dollar one year from today? Obviously, the preference is for a dollar today, because, if nothing else, it can be deposited in a savings and loan association to earn, say, 5% interest—in which case the present dollar will be worth $1.05 a year from now.

Let's change the question: Would you rather have a dollar today or a well-secured IOU for $1.05 a year from now? The answer depends on one's view of the earning power that can be generated with the dollar today. If more than 5% earning power is likely in the coming twelve months, the choice is the dollar today. The calculation tells precisely that $1.05 a year from now is equivalent to one dollar today at 5% simple interest. To say it another way, $1.00 is the present value of $1.05 a year from now at 5% interest.

CHART 4-1. Sample calculation form.

PROJECT EVALUATION – SINGLE INVESTMENT

INVESTMENT

Year	Annual Period	Capital Facilities	Expensed Items	Working Funds	Total Investment
	0				

CASH FLOW / CALCULATION OF RATE OF RETURN

Year	Annual Period At End	N.A.T. Profits	Depreciation	Other	Total	Trial 5% Disc. Rate Factor	Present Value	Trial 10% Disc. Rate Factor	Present Value	Trial 15% Disc. Rate Factor	Present Value	Trial 25% Disc. Rate Factor	Present Value	Trial 40% Disc. Rate Factor	Present Value
	0					1.000		1.000		1.000		1.000		1.000	
	1st					.952		.909		.870		.800		.714	
	2nd					.907		.826		.756		.640		.510	
	3rd					.864		.751		.658		.512		.364	
	4th					.823		.683		.572		.410		.260	
	5th					.784		.621		.497		.328		.186	
	6th					.746		.564		.432		.262		.133	
	7th					.711		.513		.376		.210		.095	
	8th					.677		.467		.327		.168		.068	
	9th					.645		.424		.284		.134		.048	
	10th					.614		.386		.247		.107		.035	
	11th					.585		.350		.215		.086		.025	
	12th					.557		.319		.187		.069		.018	
	13th					.530		.290		.163		.055		.013	
	14th					.505		.263		.141		.044		.009	
TOTAL															

INTERPOLATION

(Pres. Val. @ Low Rate Minus Investment)
÷
(Pres. Val. @ Low Rate Minus Pres. Val. @ High Rate)
=
———— × ———— (% High Disc. Rate Minus % Low Disc. Rate)

= ————

+ ———— (% Low Disc. Rate)

———— ROI

23

The form makes the arithmetic easy. First post $1.00 in the "Total Investment" box of the investment section. Then post $1.05 in Year 1 of the cash-flow section. Multiply by .952, the present value of one dollar a year away at 5%, and post the result ($0.9996) in the 5% column. If more decimal places had been used in the present-value factor, the answer would be $1.00. This calculation technique therefore has proved what you already know—that 5% is the correct interest rate which provides $1.05 a year out in return for a $1.00 investment today. We have solved for the rate of return based on a given input, output, and time period. A dollar has been invested. One dollar and five cents has been returned a year later. The unknown is the interest rate.

The form provides a shortcut, trial-and-error method of finding the column which most closely approximates the actual interest rate. As the examples become more complex, this trial-and-error method proves to be a much easier way to get to the result than attacking the numbers head on with complicated mathematics.

Example of a Calculation Involving Compound Yield

Here is another example, one in which the answer may not be so obvious. What is the interest rate, or ROI, associated with the investment of $1.00 today and a one-time return of, say, $1.86 four years from now? Step one: post $1.86 in the Year 4 row of the cash-flow section. Next, multiply $1.86 by the 5 percent discount factor of .823, giving $1.53. Try again and multiply $1.86 by the 10% rate of .683, to get $1.27. Try again and multiply $1.86 by the 15% rate of .572, or $1.06. And again, try the 25% rate of .410, getting $0.76.

The interpretation of these trials is as follows: The first trial result of $1.53 indicates that 5% is not the return associated with the above investment—$1.00 invested at 5% for four years does not produce $1.86 because $1.00 is *not* the present value of $1.86 four years away at 5%. Instead, $1.53 invested for four years at 5% will give $1.86. Thus, 5% is the wrong answer. Try 10%. Here it takes $1.27, not $1.00, invested at 10% for four years to get $1.86. So on to 15%, where the results show that $1.06 invested at 15% will bring $1.86 in four years. Close, but no cigar. However, at 25% only $0.76 is required to bring $1.86 when compounded for four years. So 25% is too high a rate and 15% is a little too low. There is a spread of ten points between the 15% and 25% trials (25 – 15 = 10), and a difference of $0.30 between the $1.06 result at 15% and the $0.76 result at 25%. The percentage number at $1.00 will signify the true rate we are looking for, and $1.00 is 6/30 of the way from the $1.06 at 15% to the $0.76 at 25%, or $\frac{1}{5}$ of the 10 percentage points, or 2 points over 15%. Thus 17% is the correct answer. In other words, $1.00 invested at 17% for four years will yield $1.86.

Earlier, the reader was instructed to start with a 5% trial and fill in all the blanks up to 40%. An experienced clerk can eyeball the raw numbers and come close to selecting the right discount-rate column the first time, though it is necessary to make calculations both above and below the final answer in order to do the interpolation. One also could redesign the form and widen it to include columns for 6, 7, 8, and 9%, 11, 12, 13, and 14%; and so on. These choices are left to the user. Once again, note that three components are involved in this ROI calculation; the investment, the return pattern, and the period of time.

In passing, it is worth mentioning that the discount factors used in Chart 4-1 are based on annual compounding rates. There is no reason one cannot select quarterly, or monthly, or other compounding periods. Chart 4-2 shows the different results obtained by quarterly and annual compounding. When the rate of return is relatively low (e.g., 5%) the difference is small, but in the 15% or 25% bracket the variance over a period of time is more significant—often 2 or 3 points of return.

CHART 4-2. Quarterly vs. annual compounding.

Annual	Quarterly	
$ 100	$ 100	
× 105%	× 101.25%	
$ 105.00	$ 101.25	value at end of 1st quarter
	× 101.25%	
	$ 102.52	value at end of 2nd quarter
	× 101.25%	
	$ 103.80	value at end of 3rd quarter
	× 101.25%	
	$ 105.10	value at end of year

Now let us utilize the form to work out three additional examples. Chart 4-3 portrays the investment of $75 in a Series E savings bond. For convenience, numbers associated with a 6% discount rate have been substituted in the 5% column.

Chart 4-4 graduates the reader to multiple cash flows and pictures the results of a $100 deposit in a bank or savings and loan association at 5% interest. Once a year the depositor withdraws the $5 interest rather than leaving it to compound. At the end of ten years both principal and interest are withdrawn. Return on investment is 5%; the small difference of 8¢ is due to rounding. It doesn't make any difference which year the principal is taken out—at the end of one year or 100 years—the answer still is 5%. We are concerned with the return associated with the investment so long as it is, in fact, invested.

Next is an illustration of a "paying off the mortgage" calculation. A $30,000 mortgage is assumed, payments are $4,471 annually for ten years, and the interest rate is alleged to be 8%. Our job is to confirm this. Chart 4-5 does so. The interpolation section is used to zero in on the correct number between 5% and 10%.

These three examples were selected for a purpose: they portray in simplified form the most common types of transactions associated with a single investment. The reason for distinguishing among them will become more apparent as we go along. In the first instance (Series E bond), the principal is left to compound and all proceeds are taken out at one time some years later. In the second case, interest is withdrawn annually, but the principal remains intact. The third example involves amortization, where both principal and interest are paid off over a period of time. The reader already is familiar with the answers; the form was used primarily to build confidence that the technique does, in fact, give the right answer under all circumstances.

CHART 4-3. $100 Series E savings bond: 6% at maturity of 60 months.

PROJECT EVALUATION – SINGLE INVESTMENT

INVESTMENT

Year	Annual Period	Capital Facilities	Expensed Items	Working Funds	Total Investment
	0			$75.00	$75.00

CASH FLOW / CALCULATION OF RATE OF RETURN

Year / Annual Period At End	N.A.T. Profits	Depreciation	Other	Total	Trial 6% Factor	6% Present Value	Trial 10% Factor	10% Present Value	Trial 15% Factor	15% Present Value	Trial 25% Factor	25% Present Value	Trial 40% Factor	40% Present Value
0					1.000		1.000		1.000		1.000		1.000	
1st				0	.943		.909		.870		.800		.714	
2nd				0	.890		.826		.756		.640		.510	
3rd				0	.840		.751		.658		.512		.364	
4th				0	.792		.683		.572		.410		.260	
5th				100	.747	74.7	.621		.497		.328		.186	
6th					.705		.564		.432		.262		.133	
7th					.665		.513		.376		.210		.095	
8th					.627		.467		.327		.168		.068	
9th					.592		.424		.284		.134		.048	
10th					.558		.386		.247		.107		.035	
11th					.527		.350		.215		.086		.025	
12th					.497		.319		.187		.069		.018	
13th					.469		.290		.163		.055		.013	
14th					.442		.263		.141		.044		.009	
TOTAL				$100		$74.7								

INTERPOLATION

$$\frac{\text{(Pres. Val. @ Low Rate Minus Investment)}}{\text{(Pres. Val. @ Low Rate Minus Pres. Val. @ High Rate)}} = \underline{\hspace{1cm}} \times \frac{\text{(\% High Disc. Rate Minus}}{\text{\% Low Disc. Rate)}}$$

$$= \underline{\hspace{2cm}}$$

$$\underline{\hspace{1cm}} + \underline{\hspace{1cm}}$$
6% (% Low Disc. Rate)

ROI

26

CHART 4-4. $100 deposit in savings and loan association: 5% interest.

PROJECT EVALUATION – SINGLE INVESTMENT

INVESTMENT

Year	Annual Period	Capital Facilities	Expensed Items	Working Funds	Total Investment
	0			$100.00	$100.00

CASH FLOW / CALCULATION OF RATE OF RETURN

Year	Annual Period At End	N.A.T. Profits	Depreciation	Other	Total	Trial 5% Disc. Rate Factor	Trial 5% Present Value	Trial 10% Disc. Rate Factor	Trial 10% Present Value	Trial 15% Disc. Rate Factor	Trial 15% Present Value	Trial 25% Disc. Rate Factor	Trial 25% Present Value	Trial 40% Disc. Rate Factor	Trial 40% Present Value
	0					1.000		1.000		1.000		1.000		1.000	
	1st				5	.952	4.76	.909		.870		.800		.714	
	2nd				5	.907	4.54	.826		.756		.640		.510	
	3rd				5	.864	4.32	.751		.658		.512		.364	
	4th				5	.823	4.16	.683		.572		.410		.260	
	5th				5	.784	3.92	.621		.497		.328		.186	
	6th				5	.746	3.73	.564		.432		.262		.133	
	7th				5	.711	3.56	.513		.376		.210		.095	
	8th				5	.677	3.39	.467		.327		.168		.068	
	9th				5	.645	3.23	.424		.284		.134		.048	
	10th				105	.614	64.47	.386		.247		.107		.035	
	11th					.585		.350		.215		.086		.025	
	12th					.557		.319		.187		.069		.018	
	13th					.530		.290		.163		.055		.013	
	14th					.505		.263		.141		.044		.009	
TOTAL					$150		$100.08								

INTERPOLATION

$$\frac{\text{(Pres. Val. @ Low Rate Minus Investment)}}{\text{(Pres. Val. @ Low Rate Minus Pres. Val. @ High Rate)}} \div = \times \frac{}{\text{(% High Disc. Rate Minus % Low Disc. Rate)}}$$

$$= \frac{}{5\%} + \frac{}{\text{(% Low Disc. Rate)}}$$

$$\frac{}{\text{ROI}}$$

27

CHART 4-5. Eight percent mortgage: ten equal annual payments.

PROJECT EVALUATION – SINGLE INVESTMENT

INVESTMENT

Year	Annual Period	Capital Facilities	Expensed Items	Working Funds	Total Investment
	0	$30,000			$30,000

CASH FLOW / CALCULATION OF RATE OF RETURN

Year	Annual Period At End	N.A.T. Profits	Depreciation	Other	Total	Trial 5% Disc. Rate Factor	Present Value	Trial 10% Disc. Rate Factor	Present Value	Trial 15% Disc. Rate Factor	Present Value	Trial 25% Disc. Rate Factor	Present Value	Trial 40% Disc. Rate Factor	Present Value
	0					1.000		1.000		1.000		1.000		1.000	
	1st				4,471	.952	4,256	.909	4,064	.870		.800		.714	
	2nd				4,471	.907	4,055	.826	3,693	.756		.640		.510	
	3rd				4,471	.864	3,863	.751	3,358	.658		.512		.364	
	4th				4,471	.823	3,680	.683	3,054	.572		.410		.260	
	5th				4,471	.784	3,505	.621	2,776	.497		.328		.186	
	6th				4,471	.746	3,335	.564	2,522	.432		.262		.133	
	7th				4,471	.711	3,179	.513	2,294	.376		.210		.095	
	8th				4,471	.677	3,027	.467	2,088	.327		.168		.068	
	9th				4,471	.645	2,884	.424	1,896	.284		.134		.048	
	10th				4,471	.614	2,745	.386	1,726	.247		.107		.035	
	11th					.585		.350		.215		.086		.025	
	12th					.557		.319		.187		.069		.018	
	13th					.530		.290		.163		.055		.013	
	14th					.505		.263		.141		.044		.009	
TOTAL					$44,710		$34,529		$27,471						

INTERPOLATION

$$\frac{4,529 \;(\text{Pres. Val. @ Low Rate Minus Investment})}{7,058 \;(\text{Pres. Val. @ Low Rate Minus Pres. Val. @ High Rate})} = .6$$

$$.6 \times \frac{.05}{(\text{\% High Disc. Rate Minus \% Low Disc. Rate})}$$

$$= .03$$

$$+ \; .05 \;(\text{\% Low Disc. Rate})$$

$$8\% \;\; \text{ROI}$$

Since the examples were only illustrative and involved personal funds, no attempt was made to differentiate between "before tax" and "after tax" results. But from here on, everything is after tax—because that is what cash flow really is.

Evaluating a Typical Business Investment

Now we move on to a typical business investment. Chart 4-6 shows a capital outlay for depreciable equipment of $100,000, plus an investment in working capital of an additional $100,000 to recognize inventories, receivables, etc., associated with the project. Presumably a detailed profit and loss statement was forecast for each year as a result of the new investment, and from this we lift the cash flow, or profit after tax plus depreciation. To keep the example simple, any investment credit is ignored and straight-line depreciation for both book and tax purposes is assumed—though one could and should change the numbers to allow for these factors. Notice that the life of the project is estimated at ten years. After that time, the capital equipment is assumed to be worthless (though salvage should be recognized in the final year if it exists) and the working capital, which does not depreciate, is withdrawn from the investment and used for another purpose.

Bear in mind that our concern involves the original $200,000 and how it is put to work. What happens to the proceeds after they return to the business in the form of cash flows from profit and depreciation is not of concern; the ROI applies to funds invested only for so long as they are in fact invested. Some may argue this point, but when paying off the $30,000 mortgage in Chart 4-5, one does not normally consider as part of the bank's return on its investment in the mortgage how the bank will subsequently use the money repaid. The return of working capital in Year 10 is like a "balloon payment." One might reason that the $100,000 in working capital had, of itself, a zero return on investment since $100,000 was put in, left there awhile, and ultimately taken out. But then one is pressed to say that all of the profit came from the capital investment in the machine. Actually, the investment must be considered in toto—one component cannot do the job without the other. In combination they make up a project, and in combination they earn a return. More discussion of this matter is reserved for Chapter 5.

Comparing These Results with Alternative Methods

Much space has been devoted to these illustrations because the author's experience in presenting the subject to others has shown that for some the concept will be new and somewhat esoteric. Yet the reader must understand it before going further.

Turn back for a moment to Chapter 3 and look at Chart 3-1. Using the same data as were given in Chart 4-6, we shall review some of the other answers resulting from so-called ROI calculations. The "average annual profit ÷ average value of assets employed" would be $30,000 divided by $150,000 (average fixed assets of $50,000 plus $100,000 current), or 20%. The "average annual cash flow ÷ average value of assets employed" would be $40,000 divided by $150,000, or 26.7%. A given year's "profit to gross assets" is arrived at by dividing $30,000 by $200,000, which equals 15%. And the ratio of profit or cash flow to net assets would vary year by year according to the depreciated value of the capital facilities. Such results are merely the division of one number by another—

CHART 4-6. Typical business investment of $200,000, with ROI of 18.5%

PROJECT EVALUATION – SINGLE INVESTMENT

INVESTMENT

Year	Annual Period	Capital Facilities	Expensed Items	Working Funds	Total Investment
	0	$100M		$100M	$200M

CASH FLOW / CALCULATION OF RATE OF RETURN

Year	Annual Period At End	N.A.T. Profits	Depreciation	Other	Total	Trial 5% Disc. Rate Factor	Present Value	Trial 10% Disc. Rate Factor	Present Value	Trial 15% Disc. Rate Factor	Present Value	Trial 25% Disc. Rate Factor	Present Value	Trial 40% Disc. Rate Factor	Present Value
	0					1.000		1.000		1.000		1.000		1.000	
	1st	30	10		40	.952		.909		.870	34.8	.800	32.0	.714	
	2nd	30	10		40	.907		.826		.756	30.2	.640	25.6	.510	
	3rd	30	10		40	.864		.751		.658	26.3	.512	20.5	.364	
	4th	30	10		40	.823		.683		.572	22.9	.410	16.4	.260	
	5th	30	10		40	.784		.621		.497	19.9	.328	13.1	.186	
	6th	30	10		40	.746		.564		.432	17.3	.262	10.5	.133	
	7th	30	10		40	.711		.513		.376	15.0	.210	8.4	.095	
	8th	30	10		40	.677		.467		.327	13.1	.168	6.7	.068	
	9th	30	10		40	.645		.424		.284	11.4	.134	5.4	.048	
	10th	30	10	100	140	.614		.386		.247	34.6	.107	15.0	.035	
	11th					.585		.350		.215		.086		.025	
	12th					.557		.319		.187		.069		.018	
	13th					.530		.290		.163		.055		.013	
	14th					.505		.263		.141		.044		.009	
TOTAL		$300M	$100M	$100M	$500M						$225.5M		$153.6M		

INTERPOLATION

$$\frac{25.5}{71.9} = .35$$

25.5 (Pres. Val. @ Low Rate Minus Investment)

71.9 (Pres. Val. @ Low Rate Minus Pres. Val. @ High Rate)

$$.35 \times \frac{.10}{(\% \text{ High Disc. Rate Minus } \% \text{ Low Disc. Rate})} = .035$$

$$+ \frac{.150}{(\% \text{ Low Disc. Rate})}$$

$$= 18.5\% \quad \text{ROI}$$

something to do with assets related to something about profit. But the true ROI is as shown in Chart 4-6.

Sometimes the "payback method" is used as a substitute for ROI. This approach concerns itself with the period of time required to "get back to even." As such, it is a useful indicator of risk, but totally lacking in value as an expression of return. Chart 4-7 shows why. Both projects have a "payback" of $3\frac{1}{3}$ years; i.e., at that point the original investment has been recovered. However, the objective of business is not to get back to even, but rather to earn a return. Obviously Proposal A is better because it provides a cash return for a longer period of time.

CHART 4-7. Illustration of fallacy of the payback method.

	Proposal A	Proposal B
Investment	$100	$100
Cash flow		
Year 1	30	30
Year 2	30	30
Year 3	30	30
Year 4	30	30
Year 5	30	
Year 6	30	
Year 7	30	
Year 8	30	

Interpretation
of Results

Now comes a vital question: What is a good ROI for an individual project? One answer is to consider the degree of successful innovation, the extent to which this project represents an improvement; the more significant the improvement, the greater the appropriate reward should be. Another way, a more tangible one, of seeking an answer is to consider the element of risk. Remember that a savings bond pays 6%, and regular time deposits at banks are in the same range. So there is a floor on a low-risk situation of about 6%. From this base the rate goes up as the risk goes up. First mortgages run about 8% these days, second mortgages perhaps 11 or 12%, and so on up to the "godfather" environment where returns are very high but so are the risks of staying alive. Like Jimmy the Greek, you can calculate the odds for success, since "odds" are synonymous with "risks." To oversimplify, a 40% ROI with a 50% chance of success is the same as a 20% ROI with a 100% chance of success, given enough of a sample to make the odds statistically significant.

Much space could be devoted to the issue of risk versus reward. It is a complicated subject, and only the bare fundamentals are touched on here. The passage of time usually is thought of as a risk; that is why long-term bonds traditionally carry a higher rate than short-term issues, unless money markets are temporarily upset by other overriding influences. Investments that are "front-end loaded"–i.e., those involving an abnormal time span between outlay and reward–also carry a higher risk and thus should project a better than normal return.

From this one might conclude that, given a choice between two projects with equal ROIs and only a difference in the life of the project, preference would go to the proposal with the shorter life. But sometimes it may be smart to go the other way. Consider this: two projects, both with outstanding ROIs of, say, 30%; one will terminate in five years, the other in ten. If it is unusual to enjoy such a generous reward and the risks are not too high, let's keep as much money invested this way as long as possible.

Another consideration is the consequence of failure. What are the practical economic boundaries that encompass the proposition? Is it an all-or-nothing deal? Or is the project virtually certain to achieve at least some success, even if less than projected? Perhaps there is a chance of hitting the jackpot—an innovation which might produce a dramatic impact on the business. In other words, what are the upside opportunities and the downside dangers? Various formulas have been proposed to organize these thoughts into mathematical expressions of risk/reward. Unfortunately, most of them are too complicated to apply in practice. Only the analyst understands what he is trying to do, and management remains skeptical. Their attitude: "If you don't understand it, oppose it." To a large extent, management judgment takes over after the numbers have done as much as they can to identify the issues and alternatives.

Clever subordinates sometimes try to "beat the game" of ROI project evaluation. A few common stratagems follow.

First, there may be spare facilities available for one reason or another—a building, a machine, unused systems capacity, and so on. Since "they are there anyway," the evaluation shows no charge against the proposed project for the imputed costs of these facilities. For example, if machine time is available, the first project coming down the pike will get it free, and a succeeding project will have to bear the investment cost of an additional new machine in order to justify itself. However, if Project B were squeezed in ahead of Project A, it could utilize the "free" capacity. One must take pains to put the numbers together in a proper manner.

Another trick is to link a high-paying project with a not-so-hot project if in combination the result still is good enough to warrant approval. "As long as we're buying this new machine, which shows an excellent return, let's at the same time redo all the lighting, paint the walls, and rehabilitate the area." The latter expenditures may or may not be directly associated with and inseparable from the machine purchase. Management must look closely to verify that projects are segregated to include only their necessary components, so that other things do not get a free ride.

Still another common ruse sometimes begins with this dialogue: "Well, boss, if you don't approve my investment proposal for a new boiler you'll shut the whole plant down, so I'm really saving the entire profit of the plant and therefore will show that as 'cash flow.'" Then, a few months later, the same fellow is back again with another crisis—for example, new electrical wiring or something—and if you turn it down, this too will close down the entire plant and wipe out all its profit. The way to cope with this is to ask the man to plan out and list *all* of these so-called necessary expenditures for the next few years. Perhaps when they are added together, it's better to close the doors than be bled to death a few drops at a time.

The list of complex investment possibilities is a long one. What about capital expenditures that can't be justified now but because of greater savings in the future may qualify next year—so why not spend the money today? What is the correct way to account for negative cash flows sprinkled through the life of a project? Does one use up available funds now on an otherwise acceptable project when an even better proposition is in sight a year or two away? All good questions, but primarily for the analyst rather than the manager. This book is addressed to the executive; it is not intended as a handbook for technicians.

Importance of Managerial Judgment

A few more observations on the subject. First, the kind of economic evaluation discussed in this chapter applies only when there are, in fact, economics involved. For example, it is virtually impossible to justify in financial terms an investment involving safety or convenience. Nor can the format be used when a proposed purchase involves a replacement in kind, such as a new fork lift for an old, worn-out one. Several methods are available for putting together numbers in replacement situations—the MAPI formula, for example—but their value is restricted. These are not genuine return-on-investment situations and therefore are excluded from discussion here. However, a good way to monitor the long-term dynamics of a business is to compare for several years the proportion of annual capital expenditures going into profit-adding facilities versus those being used just to replace or maintain the status quo.

Repeated several times in this book is a caution that numbers are the servant of management, not the master. Complex investment decisions involving defensive actions, or those having a "row of dominoes" effect, or those requiring "if to the fifth" projections, can and do stretch the capabilities of the most competent analysts to quantify everything, much less to present their conclusions clearly and say, "Here is what you should do." The responsibility of the financial team is to arm management with the facts. But the decision process remains at the top. Trite? Yes. A truism? Yes. Applied in practice? Too often, no.

Summary

To summarize this chapter: The subject of return on investment may be more familiar outside the office than in it. Everyone understands interest rates on savings, or paying off a mortgage. The very same approach can be applied to individual investment decisions on which a return is expected. The calculation form shown here makes it easy, and provides the right answer. Yet it is not the arithmetic itself that dictates a decision, but a management evaluation of the numbers as they relate to the total conduct of the business.

5

ROI for a
Total Business

THE fundamental approach to ROI described in Chapter 4 seems at last to be on its way toward attaining general acceptance in large corporations. Each company may have its own specific forms and procedures, but the basics are enough alike to permit understanding and communication. In addition, some "generally accepted accounting principles" associated with balance-sheet presentation also utilize true ROI principles where discounting or amortization is involved, as in capitalizing a lease.

But there it stops. Nearly all applications are confined to a single project or to presentation of a self-contained situation. Little has been done to extend the method to measure results of an entire business. A management which understands and applies ROI in the proper manner for individual projects is left standing on the dock when it comes to monitoring total results of the entire corporation.

Because nothing is available, alternative approaches masquerading as ROI may be attempted, with predictable confusion. It's like traveling to Canada—gasoline service stations there may look the same and sell gas by the gallon, but a gallon in Canada consists of five quarts versus only four in the United States. The real tragedy is that many managers do not recognize a basic difference exists. They ask questions like: "If we as a company approve only investments with an ROI of 15% or more (using the Chapter 4 method), why is the 'return on gross assets' (or whatever) for the corporation only 7%?" (Look back at Chart 3-3 in Chapter 3.) That kind of question is very difficult to answer, because it's obvious at the outset that the questioner's understanding of the subject is quite limited.

The objective of this chapter is to demonstrate that the same ROI method used in Chapter 4 for individual projects can be adapted to portray total results in a comparable manner—i.e., to obtain a true return on investment. While the calculation is not mathematically perfect in every detail, it is approximately correct for all but isolated extremes, and representative of actual results.

The transition from keeping score on individual projects to measuring a total business is a missing link toward which attention should have been focused long ago, and its continued absence is something of a mystery. The link itself is a simple one. Perhaps pursuit of the objective has been detoured by preoccupation with mathematical complexities. Perhaps the manufacturing executive must first become comfortable with the subject of individual project ROIs. But the need undeniably exists—in fact it is critical, because we have seen that ROIs for business in total have atrophied over the years to the point of threatening the economic viability of a free enterprise system. If business, collectively, cannot generate a satisfactory return on its investment, our way of life is in deep trouble. And we are getting close to that point. The specific justification for the above comments was documented in Chart 1-1 of Chapter 1, and the contention will be reinforced with other statistics and observations later on. But enough words for now. The next step is to review and understand the "total business" ROI calculation itself.

A Sequence of Investments

Assume you are the owner of a small business. At the outset, you projected a certain investment and certain results. We will use the numbers from Chart 4-6 in Chapter 4 as representing this forecast. One year after the start-up of the business, an additional investment opportunity presented itself, and you took advantage of it. Chart 5-1 shows the second investment. The amount is different, as are both the life of the project and the projected ROI.

After two years, the business was operating according to plan until a government inspector appeared on the scene (OSHA, pollution, etc.) and noted certain violations, which necessitated the expenditure of $80,000 for corrective equipment. Of itself, this project was not economically sound, but fortunately there were some ancillary cost benefits which kept the ROI from being negative. Eighty thousand dollars was invested and the cash flow over the eight-year life of the project also was $80,000, so the ROI is zero; $80,000 in and $80,000 out—no profit, no loss. Chart 5-2 illustrates the transaction.

After three years, still another investment opportunity presented itself and was approved because the ROI of 32.1% was so attractive. Chart 5-3 gives the details.

Putting It All Together

If one had known at the inception of the business that these successive investments were going to be made, the proposition could have been shown in its entirety at one time. The calculation form must be modified slightly to recognize successive investments, but otherwise the procedure is the same. Once again this form is reduced to its essentials; supplementary data such as detailed schedules of depreciation and profit, form number, date, and so on, can be added.

An obligation or plan involving a later investment is discounted just like future cash flows in the illustration of a single investment, and the cash flows from the subsequent investments are merely moved to a later year without affecting the result. Look at Chart 5-4. Because both the investments and their cash returns vary over time, trial

CHART 5-1. Additional investment of $70,000, with ROI of 15.2%.

PROJECT EVALUATION – SINGLE INVESTMENT

INVESTMENT

Year	Annual Period	Capital Facilities	Expensed Items	Working Funds	Total Investment
	0	$50M		$20M	$70M

CASH FLOW / CALCULATION OF RATE OF RETURN

Year – Annual Period At End	N.A.T. Profits	Depreciation	Other	Total	Trial 5% Disc. Rate Factor	Present Value	Trial 10% Disc. Rate Factor	Present Value	Trial 15% Disc. Rate Factor	Present Value	Trial 25% Disc. Rate Factor	Present Value	Trial 40% Disc. Rate Factor	Present Value
0					1.000		1.000		1.000		1.000		1.000	
1st	8	10		18	.952		.909		.870	15.7	.800	14.4	.714	
2nd	8	10		18	.907		.826		.756	13.6	.640	11.5	.510	
3rd	8	10		18	.864		.751		.658	11.8	.512	9.2	.364	
4th	8	10		18	.823		.683		.572	10.3	.410	7.4	.260	
5th	8	10	20	38	.784		.621		.497	18.9	.328	12.5	.186	
6th					.746		.564		.432		.262		.133	
7th					.711		.513		.376		.210		.095	
8th					.677		.467		.327		.168		.068	
9th					.645		.424		.284		.134		.048	
10th					.614		.386		.247		.107		.035	
11th					.585		.350		.215		.086		.025	
12th					.557		.319		.187		.069		.018	
13th					.530		.290		.163		.055		.013	
14th					.505		.263		.141		.044		.009	
TOTAL	$40M	$50M	$20M	$110M						$70.3M		$55.0M		

INTERPOLATION

$$\frac{.3 \; \text{(Pres. Val. @ Low Rate Minus Investment)}}{15.3 \; \text{(Pres. Val. @ Low Rate Minus Pres. Val. @ High Rate)}} = .02$$

$$.02 \times \frac{.10 \; \text{(\% High Disc. Rate Minus \% Low Disc. Rate)}}{} = .002$$

$$.002 + .150 \; \text{(\% Low Disc. Rate)} = 15.2\% \; \text{ROI}$$

36

CHART 5-2. Additional investment of $80,000, with ROI of 0%.

PROJECT EVALUATION – SINGLE INVESTMENT

INVESTMENT

Year	Annual Period	Capital Facilities	Expensed Items	Working Funds	Total Investment
	0	$80M			$80M

CASH FLOW / CALCULATION OF RATE OF RETURN

Year	Annual Period At End	N.A.T. Profits	Depreciation	Other	Total	Trial 5% Disc. Rate Factor	Present Value	Trial 10% Disc. Rate Factor	Present Value	Trial 15% Disc. Rate Factor	Present Value	Trial 25% Disc. Rate Factor	Present Value	Trial 40% Disc. Rate Factor	Present Value
	0	0				1.000		1.000		1.000		1.000		1.000	
	1st	0	10		10	.952		.909		.870		.800		.714	
	2nd	0	10		10	.907		.826		.756		.640		.510	
	3rd	0	10		10	.864		.751		.658		.512		.364	
	4th	0	10		10	.823		.683		.572		.410		.260	
	5th	0	10		10	.784		.621		.497		.328		.186	
	6th	0	10		10	.746		.564		.432		.262		.133	
	7th	0	10		10	.711		.513		.376		.210		.095	
	8th					.677		.467		.327		.168		.068	
	9th					.645		.424		.284		.134		.048	
	10th					.614		.386		.247		.107		.035	
	11th					.585		.350		.215		.086		.025	
	12th					.557		.319		.187		.069		.018	
	13th					.530		.290		.163		.055		.013	
	14th					.505		.263		.141		.044		.009	
TOTAL			$80M		$80M										

INTERPOLATION

$$\frac{(\text{Pres. Val. @ Low Rate Minus Investment})}{(\text{Pres. Val. @ Low Rate Minus Pres. Val. @ High Rate})} \div = \times \frac{(\% \text{ High Disc. Rate Minus } \% \text{ Low Disc. Rate})}{} = \ + \ \frac{(\% \text{ Low Disc. Rate})}{} = \frac{0}{\text{ROI}}$$

37

CHART 5-3. Additional investment of $200,000, with ROI of 32.1%.

PROJECT EVALUATION – SINGLE INVESTMENT

INVESTMENT

Year	Annual Period	Capital Facilities	Expensed Items	Working Funds	Total Investment
	0	$150M		$50M	$200M

CASH FLOW / CALCULATION OF RATE OF RETURN

Year	Annual Period At End	N.A.T. Profits	Depreciation	Other	Total	Trial 5% Disc. Rate Factor	Present Value	Trial 10% Disc. Rate Factor	Present Value	Trial 15% Disc. Rate Factor	Present Value	Trial 25% Disc. Rate Factor	Present Value	Trial 40% Disc. Rate Factor	Present Value
	0					1.000		1.000		1.000		1.000		1.000	
	1st	50	15		65	.952		.909		.870		.800	52.0	.714	46.4
	2nd	50	15		65	.907		.826		.756		.640	41.6	.510	33.2
	3rd	50	15		65	.864		.751		.658		.512	33.3	.364	23.7
	4th	50	15		65	.823		.683		.572		.410	26.7	.260	16.9
	5th	50	15		65	.784		.621		.497		.328	21.3	.186	12.1
	6th	50	15		65	.746		.564		.432		.262	17.0	.133	8.6
	7th	50	15		65	.711		.513		.376		.210	13.7	.095	6.2
	8th	50	15		65	.677		.467		.327		.168	10.9	.068	4.4
	9th	50	15		65	.645		.424		.284		.134	8.7	.048	3.1
	10th	50	15	50	115	.614		.386		.247		.107	12.3	.035	4.0
	11th					.585		.350		.215		.086		.025	
	12th					.557		.319		.187		.069		.018	
	13th					.530		.290		.163		.055		.013	
	14th					.505		.263		.141		.044		.009	
TOTAL		$500M	$150M	$50M	$700M								$237.5M		$158.6M

INTERPOLATION

$$\frac{37.5}{78.9} = .475$$

37.5 (Pres. Val. @ Low Rate Minus Investment) ÷ 78.9 (Pres. Val. @ Low Rate Minus Pres. Val. @ High Rate) = .475

.475 × .150 (% High Disc. Rate Minus % Low Disc. Rate) = .071

.071 + .250 (% Low Disc. Rate) = 32.1% ROI

38

CHART 5–4. Combined investment and ROI of sequential investments shown in Charts 4–6, 5–1, 5–2, and 5–3.

PROJECT EVALUATION – SUCCESSIVE INVESTMENTS

CALCULATION OF RETURN ON INVESTMENT

Annual Period At End	0% Disc. Rate Total Invest.	0% Disc. Rate Total Cash Flow	10% Factor	10% PV of Investment	10% PV of Cash Flow	15% Factor	15% PV of Investment	15% PV of Cash Flow	25% Factor	25% PV of Investment	25% PV of Cash Flow	40% Factor	40% PV of Investment	40% PV of Cash Flow
0	200		1.000			1.000	200.0		1.000	200.0		1.000		
1st	70	40	.909			.870	60.9	34.8	.800	56.0	32.0	.714		
2nd	80	58	.826			.756	60.5	43.8	.640	51.2	37.1	.510		
3rd	200	68	.751			.658	131.6	44.7	.512	102.4	34.8	.364		
4th		133	.683			.572		76.1	.410		54.5	.260		
5th		133	.621			.497		66.1	.328		43.6	.186		
6th		153	.564			.432		66.1	.262		40.1	.133		
7th		115	.513			.376		43.2	.210		24.2	.095		
8th		115	.467			.327		37.6	.168		19.3	.068		
9th		115	.424			.284		32.7	.134		15.4	.048		
10th		215	.386			.247		53.1	.107		23.0	.035		
11th		65	.350			.215		14.0	.086		5.6	.025		
12th		65	.319			.187		12.2	.069		4.5	.018		
13th		115	.290			.163		18.7	.055		6.3	.013		
14th			.263			.141			.044			.009		
15th			.239			.123			.035			.006		
16th			.218			.107			.028			.005		
17th			.198			.093			.023			.003		
18th			.180			.081			.018			.002		
19th			.164			.070			.014			.002		
20th			.149			.061			.012			.001		
TOTAL	$550	$1,220					$453.0	$543.1		$409.6	$340.4			$340.4

INTERPOLATION

LOW DISCOUNT RATE (15%)

Present value of cash flow:	543.1	
Minus present value of investment:	453.0	
	90.1	(1)

HIGH DISCOUNT RATE (25%)

Present value of investment:	409.6	
Minus present value of cash flow:	340.4	
	69.2	(2)

Total deviation (1 + 2)	=	159.3 (3)
Divide (1) by (3)	=	.567 (4)
Multiply (4) by difference in high and low rates	=	5.67 %
Add low rate	=	15.00
Interpolated ROI	=	20.67 %

calculations must involve both the investment and the return. The annual cash flows are merely the sum of those in the four individual investments. (See Chart 5-5.) The combined ROI for the entire package as shown is 20.7%, assuming the cash flows came about as anticipated.

CHART 5-5. Cash flows from investments in Charts 4-6, 5-1, 5-2, and 5-3.

	Year												
	1	*2*	*3*	*4*	*5*	*6*	*7*	*8*	*9*	*10*	*11*	*12*	*13*
First investment was made in Year 0 and showed cash flows of:	40	40	40	40	40	40	40	40	40	140	0	0	0
Second investment was made a year later and showed cash flows of:	0	18	18	18	18	38	0	0	0	0	0	0	0
Third investment was made in Year 3 and showed cash flows of:	0	0	10	10	10	10	10	10	10	10	0	0	0
Fourth investment was made in Year 4 and showed cash flows of:	0	0	0	65	65	65	65	65	65	65	65	65	115
Total	40	58	68	133	133	153	115	115	115	215	65	65	115

If one thinks of it as a single investment proposition, it may be a little easier to absorb the concept. If you were a bank president, and a borrower walked into your office with a request for a single loan which contained different dates of drawdown and a repayment pattern as shown in Chart 5-4, the ROI to the bank would be 20.7% on the funds outstanding for as long as they remained outstanding.

Obviously, it becomes impractical to maintain this type of calculation format when more than a few investments are involved. Then, too, actual results rarely turn out exactly as planned, and there is no way to trace all the variances and associate them with individual investments. Though theoretically sound, this procedure fails the test of practicality. A different approach is required.

An Equivalent Answer by Another Method

We begin by taking the data for a single year and expressing it in abbreviated balance-sheet form. Refer to Chart 5-6. Cash-flow data is selected from Year 4 because this is the first year in which all projects are operative. Year 5 could also be used, but Year 6 is not representative because it includes a return of working capital as part of the cash flow. In later years the contributions of some projects have expired and therefore their cash flows are no longer extant.

Since asset life, or the period of time over which cash returns are received, is a necessary part of a true ROI calculation, it is the next thing to be determined. Chart 5-7 lists the assets and develops a weighted average life, which in this instance is nine years.

To recap, the total investment is made up of fixed assets and working capital amounting to $550,000. The annual composite cash flow on this investment during the period in which all projects are active is $133,000. Cash flow divided by investment is 24.2%.

CHART 5-6. Balance-sheet and cash-flow data.

Assets	
Working funds (Project 1–$100M; Project 2–$20M; Project 4–$50M)	$170M
Facilities (Project 1–$100M; Project 2–$50M; Project 3–$80M; Project 4–$150M	380M
Total investment	$550M
Cash Flow (4th Year)	
Net Profit	$ 88M
Add back depreciation	45M
Total cash flow	$133M
Annual cash flow to assets ($133M ÷ $550M)	24.2%

At this point we do not yet have an ROI. If all the individual investments were comprised exclusively of working capital, which is returned to the till intact after the project terminates, then 24.2% would be, in fact, a true ROI. To say it another way, if you deposited $550,000 in a bank and collected $133,000 in interest annually, the 24.2% return is correct because at any time—5 or 10 or 100 years from now—the principal of $550,000 is still available.

On the other hand, if all the $550,000 were in fixed (wasting) assets, the return would be analogous to that for paying off a mortgage of $550,000 at the rate of $133,000 annually for X number of years—in this case, nine—at the end of which time there is no balance. The interest rate, or return, under such a condition can easily be calculated, as will be seen in a moment.

Since the accumulation of investments contains some of each type, it is necessary to weight out the proportion of fixed assets and current assets (working capital) and arrive at a composite. It was noted that if all the assets were current the ROI would be 24.2%; now we need to know the return if all were fixed.

A conventional amortization table provides the answer. Look at Chart 5-8. As an example, if an annual cash flow were 10.2% of the original investment (see body of table) and such cash flow continued for 17 years (see "Year"), the true ROI would be 7% (see column heading). This particular table is based on annual compounding so as to be comparable with the rates used for individual project evaluations; one could just as easily choose a table developed to recognize more frequent compounding.

CHART 5-7. Calculation of average facility life.

	Dollar Investment	*Percent of Investment*	*Years Life*	*Weighted Life*
Project 1	$100M	26%	10	2.6 years
Project 2	50M	13	5	.7 years
Project 3	80M	21	8	1.7 years
Project 4	150M	40	10	4.0 years
Total	$380M	100%		9.0 years

CHART 5-8. Return on investment: Cash flows and lives associated with various returns when principal is amortized as a part of cash flow.

Year	0%	1%	2%	3%	4%	5%	6%	7%	8%	9%	10%	12%	15%	18%	21%	24%	25%
5	.200	.206	.212	.218	.225	.231	.237	.244	.250	.257	.264	.277	.298	.320	.342	.364	.372
6	.167	.173	.179	.185	.191	.197	.203	.210	.216	.223	.230	.243	.264	.286	.308	.331	.339
7	.143	.149	.155	.161	.167	.173	.179	.186	.192	.199	.205	.219	.240	.262	.285	.308	.316
8	.125	.131	.137	.142	.149	.155	.161	.167	.174	.181	.187	.201	.223	.245	.268	.292	.300
9	.111	.117	.123	.128	.134	.141	.147	.153	.160	.167	.174	.188	.210	.232	.256	.280	.289
10	.100	.106	.111	.117	.123	.130	.136	.142	.149	.156	.163	.177	.199	.223	.247	.272	.280
11	.091	.096	.102	.108	.114	.120	.127	.133	.140	.147	.154	.168	.191	.215	.239	.265	.273
12	.083	.089	.095	.100	.107	.113	.119	.126	.133	.140	.147	.161	.184	.209	.234	.260	.268
13	.077	.082	.088	.094	.100	.106	.113	.120	.127	.134	.141	.156	.179	.204	.229	.256	.265
14	.071	.077	.083	.089	.095	.101	.108	.114	.121	.128	.136	.151	.175	.200	.226	.252	.262
15	.067	.072	.078	.084	.090	.096	.103	.110	.117	.124	.131	.147	.171	.196	.223	.250	.259
16	.063	.068	.074	.080	.086	.092	.099	.106	.113	.120	.128	.143	.168	.194	.220	.248	.257
17	.059	.064	.070	.076	.082	.089	.095	.102	.110	.117	.125	.140	.165	.191	.219	.246	.256
18	.056	.061	.067	.073	.079	.086	.092	.099	.107	.114	.122	.138	.163	.190	.217	.245	.255
19	.053	.058	.064	.070	.076	.083	.090	.097	.104	.112	.120	.136	.161	.188	.216	.244	.254
20	.050	.055	.061	.067	.074	.080	.087	.094	.102	.110	.117	.134	.160	.187	.215	.243	.253
22	.045	.051	.057	.063	.069	.076	.083	.090	.098	.106	.114	.131	.157	.185	.213	.242	.252
24	.042	.047	.053	.059	.066	.072	.080	.087	.095	.103	.111	.128	.155	.183	.212	.241	.251
26	.038	.044	.050	.056	.063	.070	.077	.085	.093	.101	.109	.127	.154	.182	.211	.241	.251
28	.036	.041	.047	.053	.060	.067	.075	.082	.090	.099	.107	.125	.153	.182	.211	.241	.250
30	.033	.039	.045	.051	.058	.065	.073	.081	.089	.097	.106	.124	.152	.181	.211	.240	.250
32	.031	.037	.043	.049	.056	.063	.071	.079	.087	.096	.105	.123	.152	.181	.210	.240	.250
34	.029	.035	.041	.047	.054	.062	.070	.078	.086	.095	.104	.123	.151	.181	.210	.240	.250
36	.028	.033	.039	.046	.053	.060	.068	.077	.085	.094	.103	.122	.151	.180	.210	.240	.250
38	.026	.032	.038	.044	.052	.059	.067	.076	.085	.094	.103	.122	.151	.180	.210	.240	.250
40	.025	.030	.037	.043	.051	.058	.066	.075	.084	.093	.102	.121	.151	.180	.210	.240	.250
45	.022	.028	.034	.041	.048	.056	.065	.073	.083	.092	.101	.121	.150	.180	.210	.240	.250
50	.020	.026	.032	.039	.047	.055	.063	.072	.082	.091	.101	.120	.150	.180	.210	.240	.250

NOTES: Figures in body of table are annual cash flows as a percent of investment.
"Year" indicates expected life of investment.
Column headings show percent ROI under these conditions, interest being compounded annually.

42

Going back to the data at hand, a 24.2% cash flow over a life of nine years results in an ROI of somewhere between 18 and 21%. On a straight-line interpolation, the number is about 19.2%.

Now to the actual weighting. Since wasting, or fixed, assets amounted to 69.1% of the total, the ROI of 19.2% is appropriate to these. And since current, or nonwasting, assets make up 30.9% of the total, the return of 24.2% goes with these. The combination is shown in Chart 5-9. The composite rate of return using this alternative method is 20.75%, a number very close to the 20.67% rate which resulted from the use of the calculation format normally associated with individual investments.

In the interest of getting the message across, the text of the past few pages has focused primarily on the *mechanics* of a total-business ROI, without digression into matters of theory along the way. Now let us take time to further analyze this calculation to better understand exactly what it tells, what it implies, and what it omits.

CHART 5-9. Calculation of composite ROI for entire business.

I. Determine annual cash flow to total assets.

$$\frac{\text{Cash flow}}{\text{Total assets}} = \frac{\$133\text{M}}{\$550\text{M}} = 24.2\%$$

II. Calculate percent of current and fixed to total assets.

Net current assets	$170M	or 30.9%	of total assets
Gross fixed assets	380M	or 69.1%	of total assets
Total assets	$550M		

III. Calculate composite ROI

    A. *Current portion*

% annual return	24.2	
% current to total	× 30.9	
Current portion of return		7.48%

    B. *Fixed portion*

Value of 24.2% annual return for the average 9-year facility life (found in amortization table)	19.2	
% fixed to total	× 69.1	
Fixed portion of return		13.27%

Composite rate of return: 20.75%

Interpretation of the Result

From a practical standpoint, a number of adaptations were necessary to get the job done. In the process, some liberties were taken with pure mathematics simply because there was no other choice. Sometimes the only tools available to the analyst consist of a balance sheet and a cash-flow statement for a given year. Since the concept of ROI involves in this instance a time period greater than one year, the calculation inherently implies that the investment and the operating results of the current period are representative of both past and future business performance involving these assets. Furthermore, the problem must be expressed in a format which contains the ingredients essential to the calculation of a solution.

Using the example above, readily available data would be those shown in Chart 5-6. The task is to put the numbers together in a manner that simulates as closely as possible the "true" answer shown in Chart 5-4. Thus the hypothesis is as follows: The investment of $170,000 in working funds and $380,000 in facilities was made all at once; the annual cash flow of $133,000 is typical and will recur each year during the life of the investment; the life of the investment is calculated at 8.4 years by dividing an annual depreciation charge of $45,000 (see Chart 5-6) by the original investment of $380,000. (Observe that the true average asset life as developed in Chart 5-7 is 9 years, but remember that this detail is not available from a balance sheet; therefore the asset life must be derived. But also note that the variance is minor.)

Once the necessary ingredients for the calculation are assembled, one could do the arithmetic in either of two ways: by using the format for an individual investment (e.g., Chart 5-1, 5-2), or by taking the approach described in Charts 5-6, 5-8, and 5-9, and related text. The answers will be substantially the same. Since the latter is much easier, it is suggested as the normal method. The procedure recommended contains a minor mathematical flaw which becomes significant only in short-lived, low-ROI situations. With a little extra effort it can be corrected if the user so chooses. Technical discussion is in Appendix B.

In practice, balance sheets and cash-flow statements are more complex than shown in these simplified examples. For example, one must take a stand in classifying certain "in-between" assets either as perpetuating or as wasting, and a variety of issues surrounding the definition of cash flow require resolution. Discussion of these necessary details has been deferred to later chapters in order to concentrate here on the core of the theory itself. At this time, diversions in all directions to address "What about this?" and "What about that?" questions would risk losing sight of the main point.

In addition to working out the particulars essential to completion of real-life ROIs, it is possible to make many other refinements to the above basic method. The author has researched several, and readers are encouraged to develop their own. A constant dilemma associated with efforts toward purification is the tradeoff between complexity of mechanics and accuracy of results. The situation is not unlike that involved in the actual manufacture of a product. New technology is constantly pursued, and once in a while an improvement is forthcoming which is practical to incorporate and which will result in a better product, or lower cost, or both. However, after several years of casual effort in exploring the byways of the basic method above, no alternative has yet been found that provides a refinement in accuracy commensurate with the extra physical and mental work involved. Therefore, instead of concentrating further on theoretical improvements, the author has focused on the pursuit of immediate, practical applications. Since these all spring from a common root, they provide a cohesiveness which is of inestimable value; a business may be studied from many angles, but the method of keeping score is consistent.

The postings in Chart 1-1 in Chapter 1 were based on the approach described in this chapter. Though the results are approximate (i.e., within one or two ROI points of a more refined answer), the deteriorating trend of performance in U. S. industry is unmistakable. Of perhaps more significance, the absolute numbers are now becoming alarming. Who wants to put his money out to risk in U. S. durable goods manufacturing with returns like these? Again, the ramifications are discussed in more depth later on.

Another look at "average" industrial results is shown in Chart 5-10. The ROIs are

CHART 5-10. Estimated ROI for 143 NYSE-listed companies, random sample, 1969.

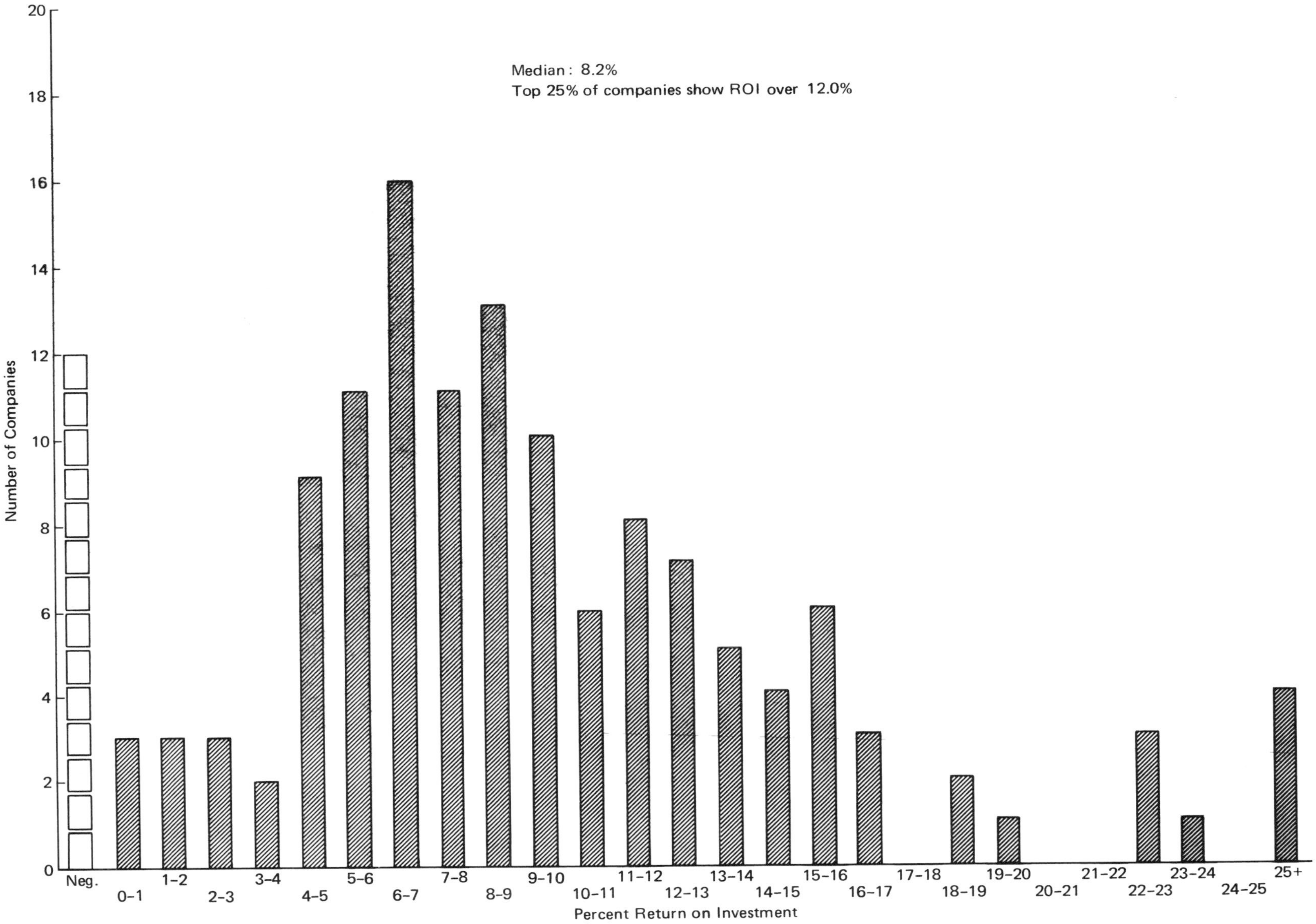

Median: 8.2%
Top 25% of companies show ROI over 12.0%

45

for a random sample of New York Stock Exchange-listed companies for 1969, a year considered to be reasonably satisfactory for most businesses. While some shortcuts were necessary in the calculations, the returns are representative and confirm that a sizable percentage, if not a majority, have not been doing very well at all. Fortunately, there still are a few big winners around—it can be done!

Determining What Is Par for the Course

What, then, is a good return? As noted in the preceding chapter, a precise answer is not possible, since judgments are required in matters of risk, alternatives, timing, and the like. But the world around us provides the parameters. Obviously, ROIs below 5 or 6% must be considered poor, since low-risk investments in various long-term government securities approach this range on an after-tax basis. Other available reference points are the prevailing and historical rates on various types of real estate mortgages, industrial and utility bonds, and so on to more risky investments such as wildcatting for oil or other highly speculative ventures.

The author's guidelines for an average manufacturing business, expressed in an academic grading system, are as follows:

ROI	Grade
13% and up	A+
11–12.9%	A
9–10.9%	B
7–8.9%	C
5–6.9%	D
Under 5%	F

These ratings are somewhat below the level usually considered acceptable for an individual money-making project. A total business also will require investments which of themselves are not directly profit-generating—perhaps a building for the home office, or research laboratories, or, as noted in Chapter 4, capital expenditures for safety and convenience. All are part of the business package, and in combination with directly productive investments comprise an economic entity.

This chapter has been directed toward defining and describing a single comprehensive method for measuring the financial results of a total business. The balance of the book consists of additional applications and interpretations which derive from the basic ROI theory.

6

Utilization
of Resources

SINCE the word "investment" has a monetary connotation, the term "return on investment" is regarded as a financial expression. But a more pristine choice of terms would be "return on resources employed." Such resources, in addition to capital, include time, technology, manpower, and materials. A prudent manager must not lose sight of the opportunities and pitfalls associated with returns on each of these. One executive summed it up this way: "Our opportunities are infinite, but our resources are finite." This chapter deals with the optimization of finite, or limited, resources, including those other than money.

A function of management is to make decisions, to choose among alternatives. Once again, assume you are the owner of a small business making three products from the same raw material but on different machines. A competent accountant has carefully analyzed the costs of production and drawn up the information shown in Chart 6-1. The issue before the house is, "Which of these products is best?" When should a manager push one in preference to the other two?

We shall see that no single answer is universally applicable; rather, each of these products is, on occasion, more rewarding than the other two.

As the illustrations unfold, one may tend to conclude that the Biblical statement of Pontius Pilate—namely, "What is truth?"—might also apply here. The executive who is forever looking for a single accounting formula or approach on which to base all his decisions should be able to see once and for all that he is engaged in a futile pursuit. Instead, investigative effort must be concentrated on the setting in which costs are found. Though the means for achieving the end will vary, the objective remains constant throughout: to maximize the return on the most limiting resources, be they investments involving money— or something else. In practice, more than one resource probably will be limiting to some degree, so the manager must combine and weight the results as his judgment dictates.

CHART 6-1. Selling prices and costs for three products.

	Product A	Product B	Product C
Selling price	$1.00	$2.40	$2.40
Variable material cost	$ .20	$ .40	$ .90
Variable labor cost	.20	.80	.60
Depreciation	.20	.10	.15
Other fixed costs	.05	.50	.15
Total costs	$ .65	$1.80	$1.80
Pretax profit	$ .35	$ .60	$ .60
% pretax profit to sales	35%	25%	25%

Pretax Profit per Day

The data shown in Chart 6-1 indicates that Product A enjoys the best margin, and therefore would seem the likely candidate for emphasis. But look at Chart 6-2. (Note: Selling-price and unit-cost data are identical for all charts in this chapter—only the business environment will change, or additional information will be shown.)

Observe that during a given time period Products B and C bring a higher dollar profit into the till. This is because their income per unit is much greater than that from Product A, so even though productivity is less, the end result is more cash in the bank. How can this be? There really is nothing mysterious about it. Nevertheless, managements everywhere have been stumbling over this simple truth for years, and rising up to walk on unaware that they had made contact with economic reality. The cost accountant's numbers are correct, but you, the boss, didn't ask him which product to push—you only asked which showed the highest percent margin, and he told you!

CHART 6-2. Same sales and cost data—Add pretax profit per day.

	Product A	Product B	Product C
Selling price	$1.00	$2.40	$2.40
Variable material cost	$ .20	$ .40	$ .90
Variable labor cost	.20	.80	.60
Depreciation	.20	.10	.15
Other fixed costs	.05	.50	.15
Total costs	$ .65	$1.80	$1.80
Pretax profit	$ .35	$ .60	$ .60
% pretax profit to sales	35%	25%	25%
Production per day (units)	100	60	60
Pretax profit per day	$35.00	$36.00	$36.00

However, the above commentary is far from complete. There is more. Look at the bottom line of Chart 6-3.

Another consideration has been introduced—the differentiation between long-term and short-term financial rewards. Product costs identified as "fixed" are those which tend to continue regardless of short-term fluctuations in production activity—depreciation, rent, the manager's salary, property taxes, and the like. On a day-to-day or month-to-month basis these are not normally sensitive to volume, though over a longer period they grow or shrink with the size of the business. Conversely, variable costs are those which are associated with the product itself—raw materials and production labor, for example. The concept of "direct costing" often is expressed by the use of break-even charts. (Since this is not a text on cost accounting, a reader who does not fully understand these comments should seek out a good book on the subject; it is a must for management.)

In the example illustrated in Chart 6-3, the $72.00 daily profit contribution of Product B, for example, comes about as follows: Sales value per day of the 60 units produced is $2.40 × 60, or $144.00. Out-of-pocket, or variable, costs consist of the $0.40 material plus $0.80 labor, or $1.20, times the daily production of 60 units, which yields $72.00. Sales value of $144.00 less out-of-pocket costs leaves $72.00. This balance left over is variously called a contribution margin, or a direct profit, or an out-of-pocket profit.

All right, so we have the facts. What can be done with them? Many times the answer is "opportunity pricing." Production time is available in the shop, so let's hustle out and bid on some business. Sometimes spot pricing decisions can be made without prejudice—without jeopardizing relationships with other customers for the same product, or violating the law, or otherwise backing oneself into a corner for future dealings. There are businesses where this method of pricing is a way of life, while in others the opportunity for such practices is limited. The conclusion: When conditions dictate, go after

CHART 6-3. Same data—Add profit contribution per day.

	Product A	Product B	Product C
Selling price	$1.00	$2.40	$2.40
Variable material cost	$ .20	$ .40	$ .90
Variable labor cost	.20	.80	.60
Depreciation	.20	.10	.15
Other fixed costs	.05	.50	.15
Total costs	$ .65	$1.80	$1.80
Pretax profit	$ .35	$ .60	$ .60
% pretax profit	35%	25%	25%
Production per day	100	60	60
Pretax profit per day	$35.00	$36.00	$36.00
Pretax profit contribution per day (direct, or out-of-pocket, profit)	$60.00	$72.00	$54.00

the order that will bring home the highest daily (or weekly, or monthly) cash contribution to overhead and profit.

When production capacity is tight, a similar tack can be employed to assist in a program of "selective selling." Business is good—there is more volume than can adequately be serviced. Something has to give. Less profitable products can temporarily be lopped off, based on their standing in terms of direct profit contribution. Obviously, decisions of this nature are very important, and the short-term financial impact must be weighted with a variety of other broad business considerations.

Material as a Resource

The data in Charts 6-2 and 6-3 implied that the limiting resource was time, and the objective therefore was to maximize results within a given number of clock rotations. Now let's switch to another facet and assume that, for whatever reason, the availability of certain product components has become a primary constraint. Strikes or other disruptions can lead to a shortage of raw materials. A supplier may put you "on allocation." Where do we go from here?

Look at Chart 6-4. If only a certain tonnage, gallonage, or quantity of raw material is there to go around, management must direct (where possible) this limited resource into the most profitable outlets. Since all three products use the same material and Product A can produce a profit of $1.75 per dollar (or pound, gallon, etc.) of material ($0.35 divided by $0.20), the choice is clear. Chart 6-3, which favored Product B, doesn't mean a thing if one can't obtain the material to make the product.

CHART 6-4. Same data—Pretax profit per dollar of material.

	Product A	Product B	Product C
Material value per unit	$ .20	$ .40	$ .90
Pretax profit	.35	.60	.60
Pretax profit per dollar of material used	1.75	1.50	.67

Still another question is in order, however. Is the material shortage likely to continue indefinitely, or is it essentially a short-term limitation? The difference is important.

Refer to Chart 6-5. On an out-of-pocket basis over a comparatively short period of time, both Products A and B return $3.00 of direct profit per $1.00 of limited material.

CHART 6-5. Same data—Profit contribution per dollar of material.

	Product A	Product B	Product C
Material value per unit	$ .20	$ .40	$ .90
Direct pretax profit per unit	.60	1.20	.90
Direct pretax profit per dollar of material used	3.00	3.00	1.00

This $3.00 covers fixed costs and leaves something to go in the profit column. The same short- versus long-term issues discussed under "Profit Contribution per Day" apply here in the selection of a full-cost versus a direct-cost approach to a course of action.

Labor as a Resource

A review of limiting resources may put the finger on direct labor. Perhaps "full employment" in your community has dried up available manpower and left only warm bodies who aren't worth hiring. Or perhaps a big new factory is going up nearby and paying wages much higher than yours, so only loyal old-timers will stay with you. Here's how the figures might look:

CHART 6-6. Same data—Pretax profit per dollar of labor.

	Product A	Product B	Product C
Labor cost per unit	$ .20	$ .80	$ .60
Pretax profit	.35	.60	.60
Pretax profit per dollar of labor used	1.75	.75	1.00

(Though Product A seems to be "winning" most often in these illustrations, the reader should recognize that the hypothetical numbers could be adjusted to produce almost any pattern of results.)

Next, a conclusion is required from management as to whether the labor shortage is a short-term problem or likely to be of more permanent duration. If temporary, the applicable numbers are shown in Chart 6-7.

CHART 6-7. Same data—Profit contribution per dollar of labor.

	Product A	Product B	Product C
Labor cost per unit	$ .20	$ .80	$ .60
Direct pretax profit per unit	.60	1.20	.90
Direct pretax profit per dollar of labor used	3.00	1.50	1.50

Capital as a Resource

Having completed this much of the exercise, we now turn to the matter of capital investment required for each of the machines making the three products, and assume each product is made on a different machine.

Capital-investment information wasn't shown on the original chart (Chart 6-1), though the depreciation numbers provided a hint. Chart 6-8 addresses the identification of money as a limiting resource. Suddenly Product C now is shown to be most attractive, though in earlier charts it usually came out second or third best.

51

CHART 6-8. Same data—Pretax profit as a percent of investment.

	Product A	Product B	Product C
Capital investment in machine	$10,000	$12,000	$8,000
Pretax profit per day	$35.00	$36.00	$36.00
Daily pretax profit as a % of capital investment	.35%	.30%	.45%

While Chart 6-8 may have some value as a guide for future capital investments, it is of no use if the machinery already has been purchased and the issue at hand is a short-term decision of whether to keep the production line going or shut it down. Chart 6-9 excludes fixed costs and relates the profit contribution to capital investment.

CHART 6-9. Same data—Profit contribution per dollar of investment.

	Product A	Product B	Product C
Capital investment in machine	$10,000	$12,000	$8,000
Pretax contribution per day	$60.00	$72.00	$54.00
Daily pretax contribution as a % of capital investment	.6%	.6%	.675%

The reader will have recognized (hopefully) that the ROI format expressed in Charts 6-8 and 6-9 is *not* the technique advocated in Chapters 4 and 5. Instead, it is "just another number"—a result of dividing one figure by another. To obtain a true ROI, assuming capital to be the limiting resource, the results must be expressed differently. Chart 6-10 points in that direction.

Now we are getting closer. Income is expressed on a cash basis and related to the initial investment. But a third key ingredient must be taken into account—the period of time over which a cash return is enjoyed. Assuming 250 days as a working year, and employing the format illustrated in previous chapters, we find that the true ROIs are:

Project A	54.9%
Project B	48.5
Project C	72.0

Calculations are shown in Appendix C, pp. 125-127.

This chapter has been devoted to explanations and simplified illustrations of various calculations related to the optimization of resources. But the arithmetic is a minor part of the decision making. Of much greater importance is the mental effort leading up to the selection of an approach. Therefore, the contribution intended by this book is to assist decision makers in organizing their alternatives into a type of checklist so as to force concentration on the real issues.

CHART 6-10. Same data—Cash flow as a percent of investment.

	Product A	Product B	Product C
Capital investment in machine	$10,000	$12,000	$8,000
Cash flow per day:			
Pretax profit per day	$35.00	$36.00	$36.00
After-tax profit per day (@ 50%)	$17.50	$18.00	$18.00
Depreciation per day	20.00	6.00	9.00
Total cash flow per day	$37.50	$24.00	$27.00
Daily cash flow as a % of			
capital investment	.375%	.2%	.3375%

NOTE: Machine A will last 500 days   because depreciation is $0.20/unit and production is 100/day.

Machine B will last 2,000 days because depreciation is $0.10/unit and production is 60/day.

Machine C will last 890 days   because depreciation is $0.15/unit and production is 60/day.

To drive this point home, consider the conclusion just arrived at: that Product C showed the best true ROI. And so it did—based on the information given. But the presentation was incomplete. No one is going to engage in a business like this without working capital, and the calculation left it out. If one were to assume inventories, receivables, cash, and the like (net of current liabilities) totaling the equivalent of 100 days' worth of sales, the conclusion changes. Product A now comes up best, with B and C following along behind. Here are the results (calculations are shown in Appendix C, pp. 128-130):

Project A	25.2%
Project B	21.5
Project C	22.1

Apologies are in order for tricking the reader this way, but if the device helps one retain the point, everybody wins. The specific "point," or role, of working capital usually is important, and very easy to overlook in a preoccupation with other numbers.

The examples in this chapter also should contain enough evidence to put to rest once and for all the notion that a "percent profit to sales" measure is primary. Spending money to improve this ratio may or may not be a good investment. In fact, it is quite conceivable that a sound capital expenditure might, as a byproduct, produce a *lower* percent profit to sales. Generalization is dangerous; analysis is essential to arrive at the true economics of a situation.

Intangible Resources

Finally, some resources seem to defy all efforts to quantify. What is the value of a stable operation? Of loyal, skilled labor? Marketing expertise? Technical competence? These also are "investments" which took both time and money to develop or assemble, even though not recognized in official financial statements. Without such resources most businesses cannot begin to succeed. Further, it is an axiom of good management to capitalize on resource strengths and work toward minimizing the effort of resource weaknesses.

One could expand even further the concept of a return on resources employed, to include matters involving the general welfare of society, or public interest, or whatever. But such a discussion is beyond the scope of this book.

Looking Toward the Future

As time passes, the approach described in this chapter will take on more and more importance. America has passed the era of abundance. As our country's—and the world's—resources are used up at a faster rate than technology can overcome, shortages and limitations of one kind or another will add to a businessman's list of problems. Whether the gap is in energy or agricultural land or whatever, and whether the deficiency is temporary or permanent, conservation in the broad sense will become a necessity instead of an option. Now is a good time to begin developing the habit of resource management.

7

Pricing

PRICING is as much a philosophical as a financial subject. Consider the following story:

> Now it came to pass, a great prophet once addressed a herd of donkeys. "What would a donkey require for a three-day journey?" And they answered, "Six bundles of hay and three bags of dates."
>
> "That soundeth like a fair price, but I have for only one of you a three-day journey and I cannot give six bundles of hay and three bags of dates. Who will go for less?"
>
> Behold all stood forth. One would go for six bundles of hay and two bags of dates, another for three bundles and one bag. Now one especially long-eared donkey agreed to go for one bundle of hay.
>
> Whereupon the prophet replied: "Thou art a disgrace to the herd and an Ass. Thou cannot live for three days on one bundle of hay, much less undertake the journey and profit thereby." "True," replied the Ass, hanging his long ears in shame. "But I wanted to get the order."
>
> —*Author unknown*

I sent this to one of my friends in sales, considering it to be the perfect squelch to his seeming propensity for "buying" business. Instead, he turned the tables and left me speechless with this response:

I sincerely appreciate the general philosophy you passed along and exemplified by the Prophet's negotiation with the donkeys.

However, I want you to know I am in complete sympathy with the donkey that took the order. Now perhaps this is because I also have large ears or possibly because I share in the little guy's competitive spirit in accepting the order on the best basis he could obtain it, regardless of the apparent odds. At least he was going to die on his feet rather than in a pen with the other donkeys and in a marketing atmosphere obviously flooded with available donkeys. Then too, if the little guy with the big ears was lucky enough to hit some fringe benefits, like a second payload or perhaps a backhaul, he would have profited by taking the order as a means of getting himself transported out of the present stagnant market and into greener pastures or a more lucrative area.

The little donkey and myself both follow the adage of: "For crying out loud, do something, even if it's wrong. Only by being active can you improve a bad situation."

Your sales manager is sitting in the office of the customer's purchasing agent. After the warm-up conversation is over and the discussion gets down to brass tacks, the buyer looks your man in the eye and says: "If you extend the terms to 120 days, prepay the freight, and let us release shipments against the order over a six-month period, you can have the business." All of these are against your "policy." Many thoughts flash through the salesman's mind—how he's doing versus quota, can the factory get the stuff made on time, will this fellow nitpick the quality, are the doors being opened to new competitive moves, and so on. If a thought about return on investment occurred to him at all, it would be surprising—and probably inappropriate. For the ROI aspects of pricing are really strategic rather than tactical.

Strategic Fundamentals

The preceding sentence is the first key point of this chapter. Perhaps the introduction to it was lengthy, but a parable may assist in remembering what ROI pricing is *not*. Day-to-day decisions in a competitive marketplace are dominated by short-term considerations—available production capacity, ability to meet established specifications, customer's purchase of other products in the line, and so on. Conclusions have to be reached and implemented *now*. My sales friend expressed it well: "For crying out loud, do something, even if it's wrong."

It is a mistake to introduce and attempt to apply ROI pricing in this environment; absence of success is virtually assured. One of the company execs reads a book or attends a seminar on ROI pricing and comes back to the office charged up and ready to go—starting tomorrow. Unless you are in a business where transactions are on a contract or bid basis, it just won't work. Return-on-investment pricing in a manufacturing business is inherently identified with longer-term fundamentals, matters for top company officers to wrestle with. Once these are resolved to point the business in the proper direction, day-to-day decisions then will fall inside the framework of a total objective.

The fundamentals will include:

1. An evaluation of the underlying economic health of your industry and an appraisal of your company's present competitive position—expressed in ROI terms.
2. A forecast of future results if current trends continue—again in ROI language.
3. A judgment regarding the likelihood and probable impact of technological improvements—specifically, their potential bearing on ROI results.

These "fundamentals" are not new of themselves. The innovation lies in expressing such a common business checklist in ROI terms. Then the connection with pricing can be seen more clearly.

The first statement contains many ramifications. A manufacturer not only is up against competitors who make a similar product from the same raw materials; he also must cope with other types of manufacturers who are selling alternative products to satisfy a common need. Thus, it often has been said that while a product price in the marketplace may not be based on your costs, or even your competitors' costs, it is related to *somebody's* costs. Dissimilar products will compete when they perform essentially the same function—for example, steel versus aluminum versus plastic for automobile components.

Most executives understand this, and will ask their staffs to dig up all available data on competitive materials and manufacturing costs so as to better evaluate their own position. But an analysis which stops at this point is incomplete and dangerous. Chapter 2 showed that costs and profits as conventionally recorded can be illusory. This applies not only to your own business but also to those of all direct and indirect competitors. What is required is an evaluation of their ROIs. How are the others making out at present prices? If no one is doing well, yours is obviously a sick industry, because over a period of time any price should—in fact, must—return a reward commensurate with the investment and risks required to produce it.

Estimating the ROI associated with a competitor's manufacturing process for a given product selling at a given price usually requires no more effort than the practice of attempting a buildup of a competitor's costs. It can be done by utilizing the basic approach described in Chapter 5 and amplified in Chapters 9 and 10.

Next, an appraisal of trends. To what extent are both my and their competitive postures viable? Specifically, can we both continue to replace our facilities as they wear out and still earn a satisfactory return? Or is either of us "milking the franchise" by squeezing the last dollar from facilities whose replacement costs would be too high to earn a fair return? What are the time factors involved? Perhaps a competitor owns a very old facility for which a replacement could never be justified, but if the facility is good for another ten or twenty years, it may be unsound to stay with him for that long. (There will be more discussion of inflation in Chapter 10.)

The third fundamental addresses the dynamics of the industry. Is it likely that technological improvements in the manufacturing process of any supplier eventually will permit a significant change in the investment required to produce a given output? If so, will more investment be needed (which tends to lock one in), or less investment (which allows more flexibility)? Does it make sense to construct or purchase new facilities in light of the present and probable future ROIs of competitors? What will be the effect of new capacity on the industry? Is the manufacturing process so capital-intensive that, once built, our facilities and/or those of others must be kept operating almost at any price in order to preserve some semblance of a return? A simulation model of the industry, even a simple and uncomplicated stab at one, should provide guidance.

Specific discussion of the pricing options available is difficult because the above fundamentals interconnect with each other and touch on so many different aspects of business scope, strategy, and resources. A general direction will be suggested by answers to the questions listed. The old adage applies: "An understanding of the problem will contribute most to its solution." For example, if you're a sick member of a sick industry, and future prospects are not encouraging, maybe it's time to "bite the bullet." Go ahead and raise prices! Attempt to ease the pain by emphasizing quality and service. If it doesn't work, perhaps the time has come to opt for a major change in corporate direction.

This book provides the basic tool for analysis (Chapter 5) and describes how to use it (Chapters 9 and 10). To play in the business game, both the resources and the capabilities of the other participants must be known. Then one can better select the corner of the world he aspires to dominate, and be more confident that the odds are on his side.

Profit Havens

The matter of profit havens also is relevant here. Is an unusually profitable product or line primarily the result of technological or manufacturing expertise, or does it reflect an opportunity temporarily overlooked by a competitor? If the latter, why not put yourself in his shoes. At what level of product selling price will he consider the opportunity attractive in ROI terms? If his executive offices were "bugged," the following dialogue might be recorded: "Those fellows (meaning you!) must be making a bundle. We can buy a machine or build a factory to make their product, and even if we have to sell it for 20% less, the ROI still will be satisfactory. At the new, lower prices we should have no trouble capturing at least 20% (or whatever) of the total market." And so it happens.

Once funds have been invested in another facility it's a new ball game. Total capacity to produce has been expanded. As noted above, selling prices are likely to fall as the competitor buys his way into a market position. The degree of price erosion will depend on elasticity of demand—the extent to which lower prices will stimulate additional usage. Everyone wants to keep his factory operating since there is no chance at all of making money when it is shut down. Price-cutting can be like a stone rolling downhill, with suppliers watching from the valley and hoping it doesn't set off an avalanche which buries them all. After the investment side has been "locked in," options for actions to manage results are confined to the "return" portion. Unless your business holds truly unique and relatively permanent advantages, pricing for maximum short-term profit—on an ROI basis or any other basis—can be very dangerous.

On Being the Low-Cost Producer

Next, a few words and charts intended to warn against a rigid or wooden approach to pricing—or to ROI, or I suppose to any subject containing an element of art.

Consider a business which at present makes everything by hand—no machinery. Results are profitable, but it appears that a greater opportunity would exist if certain operations were mechanized. A study is made and two alternatives are presented. Chart 7-1 illustrates the situation.

CHART 7-1. Investment decision involving mechanization.

Alternatives:

1. Invest $100M in a machine to save $48M annually in manufacturing costs. Ten-year life.
2. Invest $200M in a machine to save $66M annually in manufacturing costs. Ten-year life.

	Continue with Existing Facilities	Purchase $100M Machine	Purchase $200M Machine
Sales	$200M	$200M	$200M
Less costs	190M	142M	124M
Less depreciation	–	10M	20M
Pretax profit	$ 10M	$ 48M	$ 56M
Net after-tax profit	$ 5M	$ 24M	$ 28M
Cash flow	5M	34M	48M
Net current assets	$ 50M	$ 50M	$ 50M
Gross fixed assets	–	100M	200M
Total	$ 50M	$150M	$250M
Asset life	–	10 years	10 years
Cash flow/assets	10%	22.7%	19.2%
ROI	10%	20.1%	15.3%

Either machine is projected to improve the overall ROI, but the $100,000 purchase shows a slight edge. Extra money spent to squeeze out a little more in savings would not provide an additional return commensurate with the incremental investment. And so it is, based on the information given.

But one's view of business often is through a kaleidoscope. What happens if things change, as they so often do? In this case the change is an unexpected 20 percent cut in price levels induced by competitive activity. What is the new picture, assuming that units produced and sold remain the same? Look at Chart 7-2.

CHART 7-2. Competition-induced cut in sales price.

	Continue with Existing Facilities	Purchase $100M Machine	Purchase $200M Machine
Sales	$160M	$160M	$160M
Less costs	$190M	142M	124M
Less depreciation	–	10M	20M
Pretax profit	($ 30M)	$ 8M	$ 16M
Net after-tax profit	(30M)	4M	8M
Cash flow	(30M)	14M	28M
Net current assets	$ 50M	$ 50M	$ 50M
Gross fixed assets	–	100M	200M
Total	$ 50M	$150M	$250M
Asset life	–	10 years	10 years
Cash flow/assets	(60%)	9.3%	11.2%
ROI	Neg.	3.7%	4.8%

At least it was desirable, even essential, for the business to mechanize in some way, because a manual operation no longer is profitable. Strangely enough, however, the results now indicate that it would have been preferable to purchase the more expensive machine. How can this be? The answer is that more downside protection exists as a result of the greater absolute reduction in costs associated with the $200,000 machine.

Chart 7-3 profiles the ROI results for both machines under various selling-price assumptions.

A common business axiom is: "There is no substitute for being the low-cost producer." Usually this turns out to be true, because competitive conditions will eventually or periodically assert themselves in a manner to flush out of the industry those who are least efficient. The obvious message intended by these illustrations is: Consider the potential impact of changing price levels, or volume, or technology, or whatever, before choosing among alternative investment propositions. Several ROI calculations should be prepared to test sensitivity of the key variables.

CHART 7-3. Calculated ROIs at various sales levels for $100M machine and $200M machine.

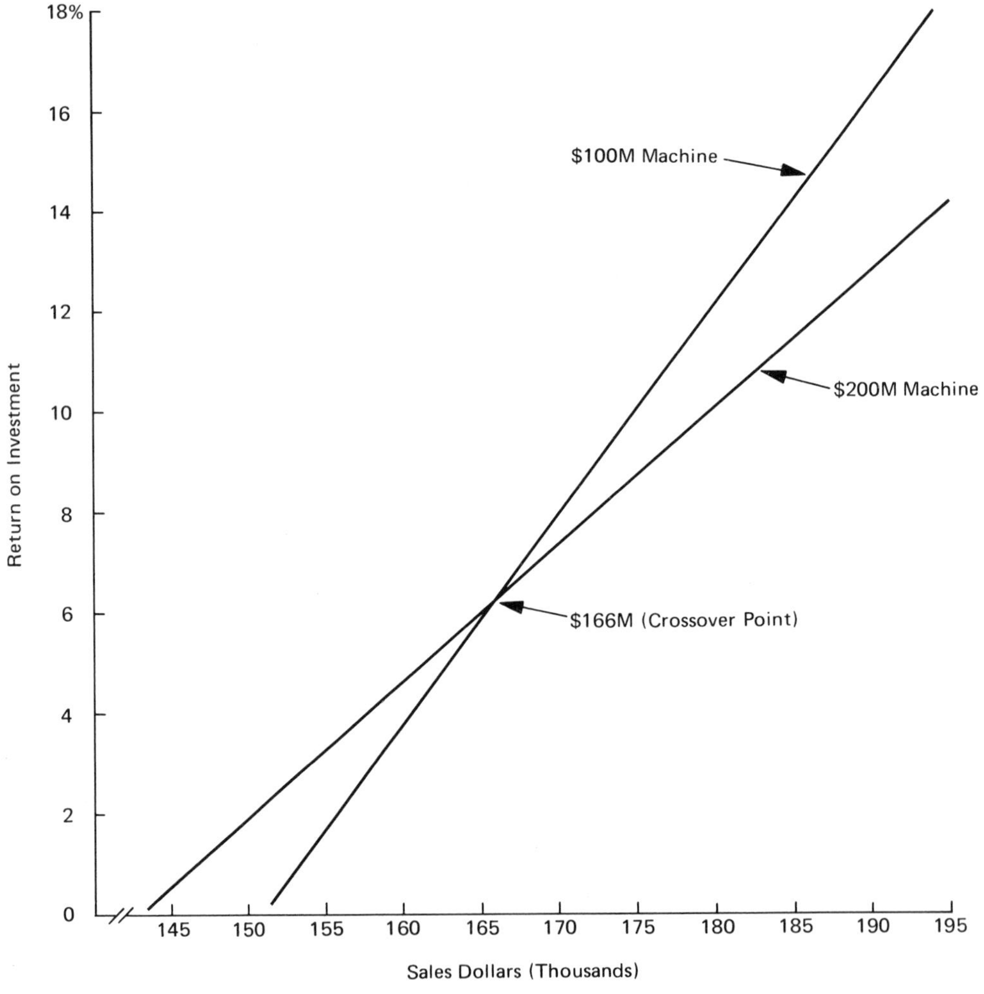

Within the framework of a strategic orientation to ROI pricing, a business may apply the concept to aid in shorter-term decisions. Over the years, a variety of techniques have been proposed to accomplish this, but most are either too theoretical and complicated or too unsound to deserve acceptance in the real world. The following approach should be both simple and useful to a job shop which solicits a large proportion of its business on a bid basis, or in an environment where a variety of expensive specialized equipment is used, or for any noncommodity type of product or process.

Chart 7-4 illustrates selected revenues required per hour—over and above manufacturing costs and operating expenses but exclusive of depreciation—in order to attain certain predetermined returns. There is nothing magic about the table; it is merely a handy way to plug into a price quotation the kind of profit number necessary to achieve a predetermined ROI target. Additional columns can easily be worked up for other ROI goals, or

CHART 7-4. Return on investment per time period under various alternatives.

	Alternative I	Alternative II	Alternative III
Investment base	$100,000	$100,000	$100,000
ROI	15%	15%	10%
Book life (years)	10	10	10
Economic life (years)	10	5	10
Annual hours (rounded):			
5-day week,[a] 24-hour day	5,190	5,190	5,190
6-day week,[b] 24-hour day	6,240	6,240	6,240
7-day week,[c] 24-hour day	7,300	7,300	7,300
5-day week,[a] 16-hour day	3,460	3,460	3,460
6-day week,[b] 16-hour day	4,160	4,160	4,160
7-day week,[c] 16-hour day	4,865	4,865	4,865
Pretax and predepreciation cash inflow[d]	$27,813	$40,555	$21,146
Revenue per hour needed:			
5-day week,[a] 24-hour day	$5.36	$7.81	$4.07
6-day week,[b] 24-hour day	4.45	6.50	3.39
7-day week,[c] 24-hour day	3.81	5.56	2.90
5-day week,[a] 16-hour day	8.03	11.72	6.11
6-day week,[b] 16-hour day	6.68	9.75	5.08
7-day week,[c] 16-hour day	5.71	8.34	4.35

[a] Based on 5-day week less a "normal" deduction for idle time due to maintenance, lack of orders, etc., or 216 operating days per year.

[b] Based on 6-day week less a "normal" deduction for idle time due to maintenance, lack of orders, etc., or 260 operating days per year.

[c] Based on 7-day week less a "normal" deduction for idle time due to maintenance, lack of orders, etc., or 304 operating days per year.

[d] This is the amount of added annual pretax revenue (before depreciation) that must result from the expenditure. The calculation itself recognizes the cash flow from sum-of-years-digits depreciation in the profitability rate.

to recognize other activity levels. Assumed is a "control unit"—such as a machine hour—which is dominant enough to provide a base for measurement.

This is how it works: Assume a capital investment of, say, $80,000 was required to purchase a certain machine tool. The proprietor considers a two-shift, five-day operation to be normal. A 15% ROI is his objective. Book life of the machine is set at ten years, but the owner has an uneasy premonition that new techniques may cause obsolescence in five years and wishes to realize his ROI within that period. (The only refinement to the calculation triggered by the latter comment is to begin to record depreciation as if over a ten-year period, but during the fifth year add back a cash flow from the assumed write-off of the total amount undepreciated at that point in time.)

The pretax and predepreciation cash flow needed each year is $40,555 per $100,000 of investment. (This number is derived from the true after-tax cash flows required, but is expressed in this manner for convenience as an add-on to costs.) Dividing $40,555 by 3,460 "normal" annual hours gives the amount of extra revenue needed each hour—in this case, about $11.72. Since the investment above was assumed to be $80,000 and the table is based on $100,000, multiply the $11.72 normal two-shift, five-day requirement by 80%. If the product is sold by the dozen, hundred, pound, etc., simply determine how many units are produced each hour and express the add-on to cost as dollars per dozen, hundred, or whatever.

Some companies employ an accelerated depreciation method both for book and for tax purposes, while others utilize straight-line for book but accelerated for tax. Thus, the annual P&L statement for this machine (if one were developed) may bear little resemblance to the true ROI goal toward which the formula is tracking. First-year reported profits will be poor if the company also has adopted an accelerated method for book, but in reality things may be going quite well. Conversely, in later years a machine will be almost fully depreciated, and an impressive P&L report may lead to unwarranted sanguinity. This situation is a good example of the pitfalls of reported profit discussed in Chapter 2.

Before leaving the above illustration, a few more considerations are in order. The narration dealt only with the machine itself. What about supporting facilities—a building, electrical or plumbing systems, fork lift truck, shipping dock, and so on. A final selling price must consider a return on these, too. The suggested approach is to analyze the ratio of investment in supporting facilities to producing equipment, and after determining a desired ROI on supporting facilities, add to the hourly return an amount to cover it. For example, if a 10 percent ROI were acceptable for ten-year-lived supporting assets because of a lesser risk, and the ratio showed 50¢ of supporting assets for each $1.00 of producing assets, then 50% of the $6.11 should be added to the hourly revenue requirement for each $100,000 of producing equipment.

Finally, recognition should be given to the average working capital tied up in the business. Assume the amount to be $50,000 net of current liabilities. A return of 10% would be a straight $5,000 annually because it is analogous to interest on a savings account. The figure must be expressed pretax as $10,000 and divided by 3,460 annual producing hours to determine the hourly add-on to costs.

A warning: Some may attempt to adopt Chart 7–4 on a "stand alone" basis, instead of as an integral component of a business strategy for ROI pricing. If done in this manner, the effort probably will not produce satisfactory results.

Reacting to Increased Volume

Another type of investment decision may also make use of the data in Chart 7-4. Though not in the strict sense a pricing matter, the ROI overtones are there.

Assume your factory is now operating three shifts, five days. Business is great, and more volume can be sold. Is it better to increase to six days and pay overtime, or to purchase additional equipment and maintain the five-day operation? Most will recognize that far more than financial considerations are involved. Are people in the community willing to work six days, and can they maintain efficiency while doing so? What about maintenance now done on Saturday? How much is gained in overall flexibility when additional equipment is purchased? Is the surge of volume temporary or permanent? And so on. The issues are many, and the evaluation must take them all into account.

Chart 7-4 makes it possible to place a "value" on one side of the scale—a financial reference point against which essentially judgmental matters can be balanced. In other words, what's it worth to you to put up with all of the grief associated with stretching present facilities and people to a six-day basis?

Assume there are now five machines. A sixth will cost $100,000. Selecting (arbitrarily) Column I of Chart 7-4, it is noted that a new machine must bring in $27,813 annually in pretax and predepreciation profit in order to justify itself. Or, to express it another way, divide $27,813 by the five existing machines and observe that each can "afford" $5,563 annually in overtime and other penalties, or a little over $100 per week. If an operator costs $5.00 per hour (including fringes) and overtime is paid at time and a half, the extra $2.50 per hour on Saturday times 24 hours totals $60.00 in premium alone for sixth-day coverage on each machine. Finally, don't overlook the possibility that someone or something may again turn the tables and replay the scenario illustrated in Charts 7-1 and 7-2.

Summary

The preceding discussion is not intended as a comprehensive review of pricing strategies per se; instead, emphasis has been on the connection between ROI and pricing. In summary, ROI pricing must be viewed as evidence of a way of life, an integral part of a total business commitment to this philosophy. Attempts to apply ROI principles only to pricing, or to other uses individually, seldom will have lasting value, as effects are quickly dissipated by non-ROI business practices. But within the broad framework of ROI pricing, it is possible to include enough cross-checks of position and bearing to keep the corporate ship on an optimum course in all but the foulest weather.

8

Measuring
the Worth
of a Business

THIS chapter will concentrate on the worth, or value, of a business. A discussion of this subject is appropriate because many executives will be confronted at one time or another with the opportunity either to buy another company or to sell their own. Often this will be the most important decision of their career. While a myriad of nonfinancial considerations weigh heavily in such a transaction, the money changing hands becomes the ultimate issue.

Because purchases and sales usually involve the exchange of stock for stock or stock for cash, it is necessary not only to recognize the value of the company itself, but also to understand the means of expressing this value through the medium of a stock price. The technique advanced also can be used for acquisition of a minority interest or, for that matter, investing in securities generally.

This is the final procedural chapter—how to measure the worth of a business. Chapters 9, 10, and 11 will be analytical—what to do with ROI after you have it (i.e., how to interpret results) and techniques for penetrating more deeply into vital financial issues.

Chart 8-1 gives condensed statistics for a hypothetical company.

Determining ROI

Step one is to determine the corporate ROI using the method described in Chapter 5. Current assets net of current liabilities amount to $60,000. There is somewhat of a predicament here: Are current liabilities a part of capitalization or not? Arguments can take either side, but this text reasons current liabilities to be merely the result of a temporary

CHART 8-1. Data on RAP Manufacturing Company.

Balance Sheet,
Year Ended December 31, 19xx

Current assets	$100,000	Current liabilities	$ 40,000
		Long-term debt (7%)	70,000
Fixed assets—gross	150,000	Equity (2,000 shares of	
Reserve for depreciation	50,000	common stock issued	
Fixed assets—net	100,000	and outstanding)	90,000
Total assets	$200,000	Total liabilities and equity	$200,000

Income and Expense Statement,
Year Ended December 31, 19xx

Sales		$400,000
Less:		
All costs, excluding depreciation and interest	$340,000	
Interest on long-term debt	5,000	
Depreciation	15,000	
		360,000
Pretax profit		$ 40,000
Taxes		20,000
Net after tax		$ 20,000

Funds Flow Statement,
Year Ended December 31, 19xx

Sources of funds:	
Profit	$ 20,000
Depreciation	15,000
_a	—

[a]Other sources and applications of funds are irrelevant to this portion of the discussion, and so are omitted.

use of someone else's money, often at no charge, and therefore are not appropriately classified with the business investment. Furthermore, those to whom the liabilities are owed—suppliers, unpaid employees, and so on—do not generally consider themselves investors.

Fixed assets at original cost are $150,000, so the total investment base, fixed plus net current assets, is $210,000. The return consists of $20,000 in profit plus $15,000 cash flow from depreciation, or $35,000. Asset life of the fixed investment is established at 10 years. As noted previously, asset life is a key element in the calculation. If one is paying off a home mortgage, the number of years over which a specified monthly payment is made will determine the interest rate, or return. Turn back a moment to Chart 5-8 in Chapter 5. An annual payment rate which is 11% of the initial amount for a period of 15 years provides a 7% return to the lender; if an 11% payment rate were to continue for, say, 20 years, the return would jump to 9%. The asset life in our present example is set at 10 years on the premise that the company is properly providing for depreciation in the stated results, which show $15,000 annual depreciation on a $150,000 initial investment, or a 10-year life. (This first example also assumes straight-line depreciation both for book and for tax purposes. Later on, the additional influence of an accelerated method will be dealt with.)

So the relationship of cash flow for this year ($35,000) to investment ($210,000) is 16.7%. Once again, if all assets were current, the 16.7% would be a true ROI, analogous to depositing $210,000 in a savings account and withdrawing $35,000 annually as interest, or return. On the other hand, if all assets were fixed, or wasting, the return would be whatever interest rate is associated with paying off a $210,000 mortgage at the rate of $35,000 annually for ten years. Chart 5-8 indicates the latter return to be somewhere between 10 and 12%, approximately 10.6%. Since a mix of each type of asset is employed, the proportion being 28% current and 72% fixed, the individual returns are weighted on this basis to arrive at a composite answer of 12.3%.

An underlying assumption is that both the investment and the cash flow experienced in this year are typical. In other words, the result, by definition, treats this sample year as representative of normal accomplishment. The person making use of this data is not bound, of course, to accept the premise; one may conclude that performance was better or worse than a preconceived norm and adjust accordingly. Perhaps it may be thought of as the score for a single hole in a round of golf—par, or a birdie, or a bogey. If scores on the other holes followed this pattern, the result would be such and such.

Sometimes it may be unfair to associate current-year cash flow with assets employed at the current year-end. If an infusion of new assets did not take place till the latter part of the period, how can a reward be expected so quickly? The point is arguable, and one could use assets at the beginning of the year—or average the beginning and ending balances—if it made more sense to do so. Normally, however, a year-end base is both convenient and representative.

Most of the above comments are merely a brief review to confirm and reinforce understanding.

A final step must be taken to focus more sharply on the ROI for the business. Notice in Chart 8-1 that a certain amount of long-term debt is included as part of the capitalization. Interest on this debt is a penalty to earnings. Were the capitalization entirely from stock, dollar profits as reported would have been higher (though earnings per share probably would have been less). Therefore, to record the true performance of the company in relation to its investment, any influence caused by the method of financing must be excluded. Pretax interest on $70,000 of 7% debt is about $5,000; after tax, round it to $3,000. The calculation is redone to add $3,000 back to cash flow. The rest of the mechanics are straightforward, so will not be repeated in detail. The new percentage of annual cash flow to investment is 18.1%, and the ROI rises to 14.1%.

Converting ROI for a Business to the Value of Its Stock

Having determined the ROI for the business, the next step is to translate these results into a stock value. This is a very important matter, because the return a business is earning often is quite a different thing from what the common stockholders are experiencing. Though these investors by definition are the owners, another dimension of value exists in the form of a stock certificate. Shareholders do not own inventories, or accounts receivable, or bricks and mortar—they hold a piece of paper. The distinction is fundamental and will be explained in the course of this chapter.

The balance sheet in Chart 8-1 showed two sources of capital: a portion coming from debt, which was invested with the expectation of a secure but fixed return; and a portion coming from equity, where stockholders were willing to take their chances and hope that a reward would be available after debt was serviced. In other words, this example involves the well-known application of leverage.

What, then, is left for the shareholder? Refer to Chart 8-2, which first shows total business results and then deducts the portion associated with debt, leaving the balance identified with equity. The ROI is then recalculated as shown in the chart.

CHART 8-2. Determination of shareholders' ROI.

Total business results:	
Cash flow (including after-tax interest on debt)	$ 38,000
Investment (28% current, 72% fixed)	210,000
ROI	14.1%
Less portion related to debt financing:	
Cash flow (the after-tax cost of interest)	$ 3,000
Long-term debt	70,000
Balance identified with equity:	
Remaining cash flow applicable to shareholders	$ 35,000
Remaining investment applicable to shareholders	140,000
ROI (based on 28% current, 72% fixed)	22.2%

It is assumed that debt financing was utilized pro rata between fixed assets and working capital, so the investment remaining after its exclusion continued in the same 28% current, 72% fixed relationship. One might argue that debt, especially long-term debt, is probably secured by a claim on buildings or equipment and therefore should be assigned entirely against fixed assets. This probably is true in a sense. On the other hand, most lenders do not look forward to repossessing an asset and tend to be influenced more by an expectation of business success which will generate funds to cover fixed charges than by the value of the security itself. Another point: The implication in this example is that long-term debt, by and large, is a means of permanent financing. In other words, the intent is not to pay it off as quickly as possible, but instead to make it work for the common shareholders by permanently leveraging the business at a predetermined ratio of debt to capital. Only short-term debt may be considered temporary, and along with other current liabilities is netted against current assets to fit the definition of "working capital." (More on the matter of leverage in Chapter 9.)

Now for the final step. What is the stock worth? Well, 2,000 shares are outstanding. Their par value, or the amount of paid-in surplus, or retained earnings, or book value mean nothing in this context. What counts is that these 2,000 shares are identified with the "remaining investment" of $140,000, so the portion for each share is $70. Furthermore, each share has a stake in the 22.2% ROI enjoyed by the stockholders as a group. Consequently, if business results are considered typical, an investor buying the stock at $70 would be purchasing a 22.2% return at that price—a handsome reward. More than likely the stock, if listed anywhere, would show a "bid" and "asked" of a much higher figure.

Next, how much higher? Look at it this way: If a $100 deposit were to buy a return of, say, 6% (or $6.00), then a $200 ticket for the same dollar return would cut the percentage reward in half to 3%. Consequently, a stock price of $140 instead of $70 is tantamount to an 11.1% return, half of the previous 22.2%. If a return of 10% were used as a reference point, the stock should be worth $155 [($70 × 22.2) ÷ 10]. Saying it another way, the price a purchaser of stock is willing to pay should relate to his own expectation of an ROI; if his ROI goal is higher, his offering price will be less, and vice versa.

To aid in making one's own ROI calculations, both for a total business and for the "worth" of a shareholder's interest, a suggested do-it-yourself form is included in Appendix D.

Practical Balance-Sheet Classifications

Previous discussion of the ROI calculation for a total company and translation of the ROI to a stock value has been based on oversimplified examples. Real-life financial statements usually are much more detailed, and one who attempts to put this method into practice will find very quickly that proper classification of each balance-sheet number into "fixed" or "current" requires some mental effort. Certain of the issues are primarily philosophical in nature and will be addressed in Chapter 10; others are essentially procedural, and representative examples are reviewed below.

Current assets Normally no problem as shown. Public accountants monitor this definition rather closely and restrict its use to clean-cut, quick-turnover, liquid items used in the ordinary course of business.

Long-term receivables Combine with current assets. Identical in nature, different only in timing.

Investments and deposits Include with current assets. A continuing return is presumed, with no diminution in the value listed. Alternatives to deal with unrecognized appreciation are discussed in Chapter 10.

Property, plant, and equipment Land is best considered a nonwasting asset and added back to current assets. Other plant and equipment at original cost is shown as fixed. Effects of inflation and advancing technology are discussed in Chapter 10.

Assets shown net of depletion or amortization (such as oil, gas, timber, and mineral properties; patents and copyrights; capitalized R&D, tooling; etc.) This is a difficult area, made so because current accounting treatment on the balance sheet is based more on tradition than logic. The absence of an identification of the original investment necessitates a makeshift arrangement. One has no choice but to reason that these assets are continually marketable and are appropriately valued at the end of each period. Therefore, to comply with premises on which the ROI calculation is based, they must be included at net value in the current-assets classification. For this reason, any cash flow from their continued amortization or depletion must be excluded from the cash flow as shown in the ROI formula. This is the only way to maintain, from a procedural standpoint, mathematical integrity.

Deferred charges Since prepaid expenses are valued at cost and not depreciated, they belong with current assets for ROI purposes.

Goodwill Present accounting standards and regulations recognize two kinds of goodwill—that established on the balance sheet prior to a certain date, in which case a company may choose if and over what period to amortize it; and that established afterward, in which case it must be amortized on a "no less than" basis. This is not the place to debate pros and cons of either procedure; both are facets of a very difficult problem relating to "pooling" versus "purchase" accounting when two companies become one. Since the issues (for ROI purposes) parallel those for depletion, amortization, and so on, the conclusion must be the same: treat as a current asset and exclude from cash flow any write-off.

Other assets (unspecified) In the absence of evidence that the assets are depreciable, include with current assets.

Current liabilities Usually clean; no problem. Classification is watched closely by public accountants. Occasionally short-term debt will be considered as permanent financing, particularly by finance companies. If so—and it's a judgment call—combine with long-term debt.

Reserves and deferred credits On this side of the balance sheet the question to be asked is whether or not noncurrent liabilities may be viewed as a part of capitalization, i.e., permanent financing. Usually the answer is negative. Therefore, reserves and deferred credits are best combined with current liabilities and deducted from current assets.

Minority interest Probably best to offset pro rata against both current and fixed assets, but for convenience may be included with current liabilities.

Preferred stock Treat in the same manner as debt (see Chart 8-2), except that fixed dividends are recognized on an after-tax basis, and so are not deductible as a cost of doing business. Otherwise the principle is similar to that for debt; preferred shareholders trade relative security of return for a fixed reward, with leverage going to the common shareholders.

Convertible preferred or convertible debt If convertible into shares of the same company, it usually is advisable to make the ROI calculation on a fully diluted basis, i.e., assuming conversion. If conversion terms are currently unattractive and likelihood of improvement is remote, potential dilution may be ignored—a matter of judgment.

The reader will have recognized that different views may exist with respect to some of the above classifications. Fortunately, more often than not the amounts in question are small, and their impact on the final ROI resulting from classification one way or the other is negligible.

Variations in P&L Accounting

Much of the controversy surrounding the balance sheet is, of course, a product of activity in the P&L statement. Transactions affecting reported income usually cause things to happen on the balance sheet. One might also say that changes to the balance sheet will affect the income statement, but most people look at it the other way! Attention seems to be directed more to earnings than to the investment required to make the business go. This imbalance is the real problem and what this book is all about, as explained in the preface. Even though an ROI approach endeavors to link rewards to an investment, it cannot fully circumvent, penetrate, or gainsay accounting entries that are essentially judgmental in nature. It is best to approach the arena, at least initially, with an attitude of acceptance of the numbers shown. In other words, by adopting the company's conclusions, what is the resulting ROI? Later on, one can make any number of additional calculations to explore various "what if" questions.

An accounting practice now common in many industries is to show depreciation for book, or reporting, purposes on a straight-line basis while at the same time adopting an accelerated method for the tax computation. In addition, different (almost always shorter) asset lives may be assigned for tax purposes to further increase depreciation, reduce the pretax profit base, and minimize the immediate cash outlay to Uncle Sam. Charts 2-4 and 2-5 in Chapter 2 illustrated this practice and its financial effect. The question now before the house is which set of figures to use in the determination of an ROI?

Again recognizing that arguments exist on both sides, this book advocates including as cash flow all depreciation, both book and tax. The total usually isn't difficult to identify. If no source and application of funds statement is available, one can pick up book depreciation from the P&L report or from footnotes to statements; additional "tax" depreciation is reflected as a year-to-year increase in the deferred-tax account on the balance sheet. Sometimes, however, an accelerated method will result in a smaller cash flow. If the business has not been replenishing its investment, older assets will have been substantially depreciated in previous years, leaving little more to charge against taxable earnings. The mechanics of this refinement are straightforward and need not be amplified with an illustration.

Accounting for investment credit involves alternatives and judgments similar to those for depreciation. Most companies have adopted a "flow through" method which assigns the tax credit to current-year operations; a minority will defer it for book purposes over the life of the asset. Again, the recommendation is to show cash flow as it really was.

In addition to accelerated depreciation and investment credit, some companies include as a part of cash flow such things as moneys recovered from the sale of assets to the extent of their book value at time of disposition.

Since no generally accepted definition has yet evolved for cash flow, the ROI analyst must choose carefully and consistently the "return" components of his calculation. This book favors limiting the cash-flow definition for ROI to the combination of reported profits, all depreciation, and investment credit. Further discussion is contained in Chapter 9.

Complexities in Determining Shareholder's Value

In addition to obstacles involving definitions, the Appendix D procedure for determining a stock value encountered several methodological forks in the road on the way to its resolution. The first fork is simply this: Should an investor in the common stock of a company be concerned primarily with the ROI achieved by the company and his stake in it, or should he focus on the dollars of cash flow applicable to the shareholder? The wrong choice may lead to an expensive mistake. Let's restate the question another way: Are funds invested in a company by a stockholder used to purchase a ticket to a calculated percent ROI, or to buy a share in a dollar amount of cash flow?

The initial step is to probe the fundamental distinction between the two alternatives; is there really a basic difference, or are these just so many words? (The reader is alerted that the following discussion will be considerably more complex than other parts of this book. There doesn't seem to be any way to simplify it. Another purpose of this highly technical section is to demonstrate that while ROI theory is basically simple, its application under certain conditions can become quite knotty.)

We shall strip the question down to its essentials and minimize distracting variables. Assume that the ROIs shown in the next chart are representative of the companies' performances; that each company will perpetuate itself indefinitely at the present level with neither growth nor shrinkage in assets or cash flow, and with no change in capitalization; that the investor is looking squarely at current results independently of dividend expectations or future price appreciation; and that the depreciation rate reflects a proper recognition of asset life. In other words, we want first to conclude how to calculate the ROI; then the discussion can turn to refinement of the results.

CHART 8-3. Example showing equal cash flows but different ROI results and different values to shareholder.

	Company A	Company B	Company C	Company D
Net current assets	$1,000	–	–	–
Gross fixed assets	–	$1,000	$2,000	$3,000
Cash flow	$ 300	$ 300	$ 300	$ 300
Asset life	–	10 years	10 years	10 years
ROI of company	30%	27%	8%	0%
Shares outstanding	1	1	1	1
Assets divided by shares	$1,000	$1,000	$2,000	$3,000
Value to shareholder at 10% ROI[a]	$3,000	$2,700	$1,600	0

[a]This is (ROI of company ÷ 10%) × (assets ÷ shares). For example, "value to shareholder" at 10% for Company B is: (27% ÷ 10%) × $1,000 = $2,700.

Look at Chart 8-3. This is a simplified repetition of the technique shown earlier for translating the ROI of a company into a normal price for its shares.

There is an alternate way to look at it—a way that could be correct, but in most circumstances is inappropriate. Refer to Company C, for example. An investor might reason he is buying a cash flow of $300 per year for the life of the investment, or ten years. Now, what should one have to pay for a ticket which assures this reward if the objective is to earn 10%? For the answer, turn back to Chart 5-8. A 10% ROI requires the annual cash flow for ten years to be .163 of the amount invested. Therefore, if an annual cash flow of $300 is equivalent to .163 of the principal amount, one can afford to invest $1,843 (.163 is to $300 as 1.00 is to X). This assumes, of course, that the $300 annual return includes a payoff of both interest and principal. After ten years, it's all over.

On the surface, the logic would seem to fit, since Company C is utilizing a wasting asset, one that will be fully depreciated or exhausted at the end of the period. And the reasoning would be proper if, but only if, the subtle remark that "it's all over" after ten years were true. However, this statement was contradicted earlier in a basic assumption that the business would perpetuate itself indefinitely at the present 8% ROI level. In order for it to do so, $200 of the $300 annual cash flow sooner or later must be reinvested to replenish the assets which are wasting. Thus, because liquidation is not assumed, the $1,600 value shown on the chart for a 10% ROI is preferred over the $1,843 amount given above as a requirement for 10% ROI under liquidation. (Mentally put in storage for a moment the question of what happens to the implied $100 profit under the assumption of no growth.) In other words, reinvestment is presumed to go on continually, and each time there is a reinvestment, the result is an 8% ROI. Funds invested are earning 8% so long as they are in the stream of business activity, and the intent is to perpetuate this condition.

The pitfalls of considering cash flow alone can be illustrated more clearly by using an extreme example. Refer to Company D. Here, too, a $300 annual cash flow is recorded, and one might repeat the previous exercise and suggest that a ticket to this cash flow also is worth $1,843. But Chart 8-3 shows clearly that the company isn't making any money; the ROI is zero since the only source of cash flow is depreciation, with nothing in the form of profit or a return. Thus, while this business might continue indefinitely by using cash flow from depreciation to replenish fixed assets, it is only spinning its wheels; there is no conceivable way to argue that a return of any kind is being earned. Even if a single dollar could buy the entire company, there's nothing in it for an investor who is obligated, as a condition of his purchase contract, to perpetuate the business. Only in liquidation is there a possibility of return to an investor who paid something less than $3,000 for $300 annual cash flows for ten years (or a shorter period if the asset already is partly worn out).

Sometimes companies are purchased with the objective of selling off the assets, or investments are made which are inherently self-liquidating. For example, a group is formed to drill a single oil well, or purchase a racehorse, or whatever. Then the *only* correct way involves the theory which gave the $1,843 answer for Company C. But if the investor expects the enterprise to be perpetuated, he is advised to assume that his stake in the company is best represented by a share of the ROI the company is achieving.

In summary, the first fork in the road is to recognize that cash flow by itself can be a misleading statistic both to the company and to the shareholder; unless liquidation is intended, cash flow must be related to an investment and the result expressed as a calculated return. If this fundamental is not yet clear, look again at Chart 8-3. Each of the four companies has recorded an annual cash flow of $300. Assuming a continuing business, are they all "worth" the same total amount? Obviously not!

Adjusting Company ROI
to Shareholder Value

The above discussion concentrated on demonstrating why cash flow unrelated to an asset base usually is a misleading measure, both for the business itself and as a basis for translation to a shareholder value. It was implied that the asset-related ROI result is a proper starting point. Now we shall explore in more depth this way of doing things.

Two ROIs were shown in Chart 8-3, one for the company and another which factored the shareholder's stake to a 10% level.* We begin with the premise that the ROI result for the company is correct as shown, since Chapters 4 and 5 built up to that conclusion. And there should be no disagreement that the shareholder also has some stake in whatever ROI the company is earning. But another decision is faced when comparisons are attempted among several companies achieving different results, or when one wishes to determine a higher or lower price to pay for a company in order to adjust to a 10% level (for example) when actual results differ from this figure. Efforts to equate become mathematically difficult, and the technique advocated here is presented more as an approach than as a precise answer. It is in the translation to a common reference point of value that the going gets rough.

Look again at Company C. The return of 8% on these depreciable assets presupposes that a certain amount of the cash flow is used to amortize the principal while the balance is applied as interest, or a return. An improvement in cash flow of 25% does not in fact increase the ROI by 25% (i.e., from 8 to 10%). Conversely, neither does a reduction of 20% in the investment base while maintaining the same cash flow really increase the ROI from 8 to 10%. Why? Because cash flow includes both interest and principal. Increasing the total payment by a certain percentage has no effect on the principal; instead, the

*The 10% number, of itself, has no significance other than serving as an arbitrary reference point—a common denominator of value. To say it another way, what must the price be to provide a uniform return in each instance, be it 10%, 9%, 11%, or any number?

entire amount goes against the interest, or return. The same situation applies for Company B, which showed a 27% corporate return factored down to a shareholder price at 10%.

The dilemma above occurs only to the extent that fixed assets are involved. There is no problem with Company A, whose assets are all current. Here it is perfectly in order to factor a 30% return down to 10% by increasing proportionally the price paid. In other words, if $1,000 will buy a ticket to a $300 perpetual annual cash flow (30% ROI) while still preserving the initial investment of $1,000, then a $3,000 price for the same $300 annual cash flow effectively reduces the return to 10%.

Returning to the problem with fixed assets, there may appear to be an alternate way out—but it brings one full circle, back to the liquidation assumption. Refer to Chart 5-8. Company C's annual payment rate of .149 of the principal will amortize an investment over ten years and return 8%; to attain 10%, an annual amount equal to .163 of the principal is required. The increase from .149 to .163 dictates that annual cash flow be raised from $300 to $328 ($300 is to .149 as X is to .163). Since we cannot raise the cash flow, the same result must be obtained by reducing the investment base from $2,000 to a lower figure. Therefore, if $328 is associated with a $2,000 investment to bring back 10%, then $300 must be associated with $1,843 to get the same percentage result. A similar calculation on Company B would also show a shareholder value at 10% of $1,843, a number considerably lower than that indicated; and the same answer would apply to Company D, which is worth nothing except in liquidation.

Here are some additional reasons why the alternate method is not preferred in this context:

1. Philosophically one can argue that investor orientation to the company is focused exclusively on the return itself—8% for Company C, for instance. How the company achieves this goal is, in a sense, irrelevant. Operations are shadows behind a curtain—fixed and current assets mingling about, things called profit and cash flow being displayed from time to time. But totally overriding is the fact that the company is earning an 8% ROI—somehow, some way, with whatever mix of current and fixed assets they have chosen. In that sense, the investor is detached from operations, rather than being a participant or partner in the specific types of assets used to realize the 8%. From his viewpoint, the goal is simply a perpetual result at this level, perpetual in the sense of a continuing return or yield on a current asset as in Company A. If he considers an 8% result too low, the price he is willing to pay will proportionally decline in the manner shown in Chart 8-3.

2. When a restraint imposed in the initial hypothesis is removed—the restraint which forbade a reinvestment of the return to gain a compounding effect—relative attractiveness to the investor changes. More discussion of this matter will take place later, but the end result is to enhance the attractiveness of an already good return by continuing to compound results at that rate; on the other side, a poor return is made less attractive. The proposed method of translating ROI to shareholder value gives more recognition to the potential "plus" from anticipated future growth of the company at a relatively rapid rate, by placing a higher value on its stock than the alternate method would dictate. Conversely, it more steeply discounts poor performance, which makes sense because of the tendency for failure to breed failure, a nominal corporate ROI being virtually worthless at any price. In other words, a stock (or company) for sale at a price low enough to provide a "good" ROI to the investor usually will be of little value unless the company itself is earning a respectable ROI.

3. Understanding the subject—a prerequisite to use—is considerably easier with the method originally proposed than with the alternate method. How many highly mathematical subjects—simulation of a business, model building, scheduling, and so on—have failed to come into common use because their proponents insisted on addressing and resolving every theoretical issue prior to implementation? By then, only a few technicians (who may still have been arguing among themselves) knew what they were trying to do. Management long since had been left behind in the process of understanding, and probably had cooled on the subject. Excessive complexity will make an implementation attempt so formidable as to discourage all but the most dedicated. The approach to ROI herein recommended has included a willingness to trade off any final degree of precision for practical, here-and-now value. The problem of a long-term declining ROI trend in U. S. industry (see Chapter 1) is too serious to ignore any longer, and a straightforward method of calculating ROI may make the concept accessible to managers who would otherwise dismiss the subject as too technical.

At this point, a brief summary may be helpful. After Chart 8-3 was displayed, the discussion pursued the question of "buying cash flow" at a price and concluded that such an approach was unsound except when liquidation of the company was anticipated. This is because cash flow cannot be divorced from the assets employed to generate it. Then attention was focused on "buying an ROI," and on the changes in stock value, or purchase price, that occur when the desired percentage return to the investor is varied from that earned by the company.

Where Does Profit Fit In?

A few more things need to be said about the basics of expressing corporate ROI in terms of an investor's value. Chart 8-4 is a reproduction of Chart 8-3 with certain information added—namely, reported profit of the companies and value to shareholders at selected price/earnings ratios and cash-flow multiples.

The profit figure was there all the time, of course; it just wasn't shown earlier, to keep an already complex discussion from becoming more so. A flash of memory may have been triggered by this number. Here now is the question mentally "put in temporary storage" a few pages back. Why not consider the profit as an ROI? Company C, after all, earned $100. Isn't this a return of some kind?

The answer is "yes and no," but mostly "no." More work needs to be done, but that should not prevent us from using what we know. Hopefully this book will serve to stimulate research to advance and refine the techniques here introduced. The answer for the moment to the question of whether profit should be used as a return is this: Neither the company's fortunes nor the translation to an investor's value is best expressed as an annual profit, because we are not buying profit dollars per se. Rather, *the business is generating an annual stream of cash flows that are related to the capital employed to produce them.* Further, it is not only the cash flow (or profit) itself that is significant, but also *when* it is realized—now or later. Remember Chapter 4 and the principle of discounting. A dollar today is worth more than the promise of a dollar in the future, and so on. Did the profit shown represent a prompt return after the investment was made, or a reward some time later? Unless an ROI approach is used, this vital issue is obscured. Then, too, a fundamental observation in this book is that the meaningfulness of reported profit in recent years has been eroded by many artificial and transient influences such as depreciation

CHART 8-4. Example showing equal cash flows but different ROI results and different values to shareholder (same as Chart 8-3, but amplified).

	Company A	Company B	Company C	Company D
Net current assets	$1,000	–	–	–
Gross fixed assets	–	$1,000	$2,000	$3,000
Reported profit	$ 300	$ 200	$ 100	–
Cash flow	$ 300	$ 300	$ 300	$ 300
Asset life	–	10 years	10 years	10 years
ROI of company	30%	27%	8%	0%
Shares outstanding	1	1	1	1
Assets divided by shares	$1,000	$1,000	$2,000	$3,000
Value to shareholder at 10% ROI	$3,000	$2,700	$1,600	0
Value to shareholder at price/earnings ratio of 10	$3,000	$2,000	$1,000	0
Value to shareholder at 10X multiple of cash flow	$3,000	$3,000	$3,000	$3,000

practices, tax laws, and a wide latitude in "generally accepted accounting principles." Finally, profit is a number oriented exclusively to the shareholder, because reported profit is affected by the way the business has been financed, i.e., the relative importance of debt. All these are reasons why cash flow (as defined earlier) provides a better measuring stick than profit. But remember that, except under liquidation, cash flow provides a useful base only when related to an investment and re-expressed as an ROI.

How to Recognize Compounding of Growth

In the previous examples, the objective was to reach a conclusion as to the worth of a company, then to appraise this value from the shareholder's viewpoint. To at least partially simplify this complex subject, an arbitrary assumption was imposed to the effect that future results would be carbon copies of the current year; that is, there would be no compounding of either cash flow or the investment. What happens, then, if that abnormal restriction is removed and growth is assumed?

Conclusions arrived at through research by the author are tentative rather than dogmatic. Both logic and mathematics can become quite involved, and, without apology, such is not the intent of this book. Furthermore, the greatest challenge in projecting the future rests not in the complexity of the mathematics but in the foresight of the person making the predictions. He must consider not only "What is likely to occur?", but also "What are the odds?" and "What are the alternative possibilities?" Management judgment must take over when the manipulation of numbers no longer provides clear direction. Consider, too, some of the other variables: Is the ROI now being experienced likely to continue, or decline, or increase? Will current rewards be plowed back and compounded, or paid out, or some of each? How far ahead can future results be intelligently projected? The number of combinations is infinite. Also, the shareholder must consider whether or not the ultimate intent is to sell his interest or to liquidate the business—there is a difference. And what about the company's future capitalization—growth through more debt, more shares issued, or both—and in what proportion?

The basic approach suggested for all this is to utilize the investment-justification procedure described in Chapter 4. First, how much money is involved in the initial outlay? Second, are any cash returns flowing back to the investor during the course of the investment? And third, what is the whole thing going to be worth five years out, or whatever?

The last question probably is the most important. In order to answer it, one must first project the business results for the fifth year ahead, not only in terms of profit or cash flow, but on the ROI basis explained in the first section of this chapter. Once a future projected value to the shareholder is determined, one can assume that another prudent buyer would pay that price for the ongoing business if the original investor wanted out.

Chart 8-5 illustrates the technique. The statistics are for the same four companies shown in Chart 8-3, but five years later. It is assumed—though not essential to the arithmetic—that all cash flows during the five-year interval have been reinvested, both to replace assets at the rate they are being depreciated and to expand the business; and that the ROIs on both the original investment and the new money plowed back continue at the rates shown on the original chart.

The "alternate method" is the one which was discussed under "Adjusting Company ROI to Shareholder Value" and which then was not recommended for normal calculations. Now we shall see why. Go back to Chart 4-1 and note that a "worth" five years away must be multiplied by .621 to discount it back to today's value at 10 percent. (As stated previously, the 10% number was selected somewhat arbitrarily but intended to represent an average real-world expectation under conditions of relatively modest business risk.) If the "alternate" ROI values for Companies B and C five years in the future are so discounted, the current values become $4,586 × .621 = $2,848 for B, and $2,352 × .621 = $1,460 for C. These results are reasonably close to both the relative and absolute values

CHART 8-5. Example of shareholder ROI—Same companies as in Chart 8-3 but five years later, with interim growth compounded at same rate.

	Company A	Company B	Company C	Company D
Net current assets	$ 3,713	—	—	—
Gross fixed assets	—	$2,488	$2,552	$3,000
Cash flow	$ 1,114	$ 746	$ 383	$ 300
Asset life	—	10 years	10 years	10 years
ROI of company	30%	27%	8%	0%
Shares outstanding	1	1	1	1
Assets divided by shares	$ 3,713	$2,488	$2,552	$3,000
Value to shareholder at 10% ROI (original method)	$11,139	$6,718	$2,042	0
Value to shareholder at 10% ROI (alternate method)	$11,139	$4,586	$2,352	0

established initially under the recommended method shown in Chart 8–3, namely, $2,700 for B and $1,600 for C. In other words, the alternate method implies eventual liquidation of the investment sometime in the future, while the recommended method is associated with indefinite compounding. Therefore the procedure originally recommended involves a combination of the two—an assumption that results for a given year will continue and be compounded at that rate, but eventually one's chips will be cashed in. The ultimate cash-in value discounted back to the present parallels the values established under the recommended method. *Expressed another way, ultimate liquidation by the investor as a result of selling his investment is a logical expectation, but liquidation of the company usually is not.*

A final look. Notice that Company D still isn't worth anything, because it has earned nothing and instead remains in the ranks of the "living dead." On the other hand, Company A is shown to have a much greater value than was arrived at by any of the previous methods. To the extent that this technique is utilized, one is advised to recognize the phenomenon as it applies to companies whose assets are primarily current, or nonwasting.

This ends the rather complicated technical portion of the chapter. Our excursion into the wild blue yonder of ROI was addressed to those inclined to pursue in depth the logic behind the method recommended for translating ROI results to a stock value, as shown on the do-it-yourself form in Appendix D.

Comparison of ROI with Conventional Ways of Appraising Corporate Results

Let us wrap up this discussion by relating the material covered so far to some of the measures of performance in common use. The picture may be much clearer in this perspective than on a stand-alone, abstract basis.

Return on equity This commonly used expression contains two traps, and it's hard to tell which is the worse. Either the numerator (return) or the denominator (equity) can be and often is synthetic. "Return" in this definition is synonymous with "profit." Chapter 2 discussed at length the problems of profit as reported, so there is no need for repetition. With "equity" as the denominator, the risk/reward impact of leverage associated with debt financing is totally ignored. Furthermore, return on equity, though ostensibly related to the interest of the shareholder, does nothing to assist him in placing a value on his portion of ownership. So the company earned $X\%$; but what is the stock worth?

Return on invested capital Here, too, are two traps to snare the unwary. Return is again identified with profit, and the dangers are the same as just described. "Invested capital" usually means long-term debt plus capital stock (though when used by rate-making bodies for public utilities the definition is amended in various ways). Since invested capital considers fixed assets net of depreciation, the result can be significantly affected by the age of the assets being measured. An old facility may show a fine return because of "milking the franchise," while a new and truly more efficient business may fare poorly under this method of scorekeeping. Finally, there is nothing in the answer to translate the value of a given return on invested capital to a worth of the stock from the proprietor's viewpoint.

Cash flow per share A moment's reflection should quickly show up a major flaw in this measure. Like so many things, it contains some truth, but just enough to be dangerous. The right horse (cash flow) is hitched to the wrong wagon (per share). Just about every page of this book refers to cash flow, but the denominator is investment, investment, investment—not equity or total capitalization at depreciated value. Think of two companies—one with a heavy requirement for manufacturing facilities, the other with most of its money in receivables, inventories, and the like. Of course the company with high fixed assets will tend to have a better cash flow, other things being equal, for the simple reason that depreciation of itself provides cash. But this doesn't make the final result automatically better. Depreciation money must be earmarked for replacement if the company is to stay in business. And with inflation, technological obsolescence, and the timing of replacement needs to cope with, one needs an exceptionally incisive view to interpret a cash-flow number without relating it to an investment base. Next, the "per share" denominator once again ignores debt and its associated leverage. Finally, no means of translation exists to express the result in terms of shareholder worth.

Book value per share This expression is quite different from the three previous ones. It is not a dynamic number, in that the "return" component is totally ignored. Instead, comparisons usually are between the net per-share value of the stockholder's investment and the going market price of the stock. When securities of a company are trading below book value of the stock, the inference is that a bargain might exist. Usually this view is myopic. Unless one expects to liquidate the business by selling off at a profit the assets purchased at a "sale" price, there are fewer quicker roads to ruin than buying stocks discounted from book value. Think about it a moment. Look back at Company D on Chart 8–3. Other than from a liquidation standpoint, this company isn't worth anything. Why? Simply because it's not earning anything.

Sometimes book values themselves are thought to be understated; the assets really are worth more. This, too, is indefensible logic, because then the economic ROI is less than that stated. If the assets of Company D on Chart 8–3 were truly worth more, the return in an economic sense would be negative; cash flows aren't even sufficient to perpetuate the treadmill. With this company, the only hope is that either new management or acquisition by another company will provide talent to take advantage of these discounted assets and put them to work more profitably.

What about corporate repurchase of its own shares? In-depth discussion is outside the scope of this book, but two thoughts are offered. First, a decision should be made on considerations other than the relation of present market price to book value. Second is a generalization that repurchase will tend to be desirable if the ROI on funds reinvested is expected to be less than that associated with the acquisition of shares.

To sum up, book value means nothing by itself; it must be related to earning power to reach an intelligent conclusion.

Price/earnings ratio Other than the ROI approach advocated in this book (of course!), P/E probably comes closer than other measures to being a representative barometer of shareholder value. Investment is ignored, as are the methods of financing, and interpretation of "earnings" presents the difficulties described earlier. But there is a hint of ROI in the expression of price, or value, as a multiple of earnings.

Conclusion

This chapter is not intended as a short course in how to beat the stock market. That, too, is another subject far beyond the scope of these writings. But if one subscribes to an approach emphasizing innate value, ROI comes closer to providing the ingredients for intelligent analysis than any other method. It is entertaining to read the views of security analysts and investment advisers as they switch back and forth from one measure of progress or worth to another, groping for a formula that somehow will lead an investor along the path to prosperity. Such activities are left to others. We shall hew to the line and confine the discussion to ROI, which has enough ramifications of its own to deserve undivided attention.

9

Analyzing
the Return

THIS book is intended to light a candle—to illuminate the difficulties of financial management under today's scorekeeping practices; to emphasize the critical need for immediate action to reverse a long-term trend of deteriorating ROI results; and to offer blueprints for a comprehensive program to do so. The remaining chapters will explore these subjects in greater depth.

It is truly surprising that so little has been done over the years to research, define, and apply the ROI concept to industrial management. Most accounting and financial principles and practices have been long since studied, debated, and standardized to some generally accepted (albeit tentative) conclusion. But only the shoreline of ROI has been explored. The effect is akin to navigating with a sixteenth-century Spanish map of North America; many features were distorted, deduced, based on hearsay, or totally omitted. More expeditions are needed to search out, understand, and evaluate ROI so that generally accepted charts are available here, too, for those who steer the course of business.

We now take leave of the mechanics of ROI and address the results. What does ROI tell about a business? What makes the numbers behave as they do? If management is going to manage this way, it must understand how to read the dials as well as how to turn the knobs. The executive's control box contains many knobs and dials, and one of the biggest advantages of ROI lies in its capacity to penetrate all the financial corners, to permeate every economic decision, to become a way of life in terms of both making things happen and appraising the results.

Some parts of the next two chapters will paraphrase earlier comments. The attempt is to pull everything together so as to understand the whole in addition to the pieces.

Readers of this book will have diverse backgrounds, varying exposure to financial matters, and different interests in the use of the material. There is no way to avoid being too technical for some and too elementary for others. The author is attempting to "play it down the middle."

**Redefining
the Return**

As stated in Chapter 3, confusion in the definition of ROI undoubtedly has been one of the main reasons it is not yet a generally accepted measure of performance (another being the absence of suitable mechanics for application to total business results). To better understand the dial marked "return," it is best to put aside reliance on accounting terminology and instead focus on a pristine expression of the term—namely, a reward in return for a commitment of resources. The analogy of "interest" was used earlier to recast the business scene to a simplistic environment. But somewhere along the line one must cope with the world of accounting and test the fundamental definition against conventional financial terms, many of which have similar sounds but different meanings. When this subject was touched on earlier, the reader was obliged to accept every conclusion given as a premise; by now he should have enough background to make his own judgments.

Prior to 1971, audited financial statements did not have to include more than a balance sheet and a profit and loss report. A source and application of funds statement, though encouraged by a 1963 Opinion of the Accounting Principles Board, was not mandatory. The absence of a "funds" statement spelled bad news for the analyst trying to put together an ROI, because some key ingredients (depreciation, deferred taxes, etc.) may not otherwise have been separately detailed. Since 1971, however, a "Statement of Changes in Financial Position" has become essential to certification by the public accounting profession. In other words, where did the cash come from and where did it go? The content and general format is specified, but considerable latitude is permitted in the manner of presentation. Because the report is a summary of "cash in and cash out," without any pretext of a connection with ROI, one must search through the listing for the key ingredients of a return or reward. Usually the significant numbers are there somewhere, thanks to the requirement that disclosure be in detail.

Some components of "cash in and cash out" are easy to include or exclude from ROI. Obviously profit is a part of the return, and routine changes in working capital are not. An often-used subtotal of "funds provided from operations" might suggest a return of some kind, but the definition varies and must be scrutinized. The term "cash flow," which has been used loosely in this book, also is variously defined. Again, the point is: Which of these inflows represent a true reward, and which are merely moneys flowing to and fro as a result of other influences? Actually, the term "cash flow" seems to be looked on with some disdain, since an official opinion of the Accounting Principles Board "strongly recommends that isolated statistics of . . . cash provided from operations, especially per-share amounts, not be presented in annual reports to shareholders." But security analysts certainly use the term a lot anyway!

As a review, exactly what is needed to calculate return? Let's go down the list again briefly:

1. *Profit.* Definitely a necessary figure, but remember that many practices are available to move this number around. Without elaborating further, if the reader doesn't

support the accounting methods used by the company in reporting results, let him make whatever adjustments he considers appropriate to arrive at an acceptable "profit."

2. *Book depreciation.* Under conventional accounting, depreciation is not a component of a return. Rather, it's just the opposite—a cost of doing business. But it isn't a cash cost because the cash actually was spent earlier. In years subsequent to the investment, depreciation actually "saves" cash by lowering the profit base on which taxes are paid. The enigma is that rules of accounting (and the IRS) don't count initial outlays for capitalized facilities as an expense, but piece out the cost over a period of time as the assets are utilized. On the other hand, ROI economics specify that all funds invested be so recognized immediately (the money was paid out, wasn't it?) and the true cash flows associated with that investment be counted as they occur in future years. For a refresher, review Chart 2-3.

This book has no quarrel with the accounting treatment—there's no practical alternative conceptually. But for ROI purposes, the question is just as basic: How much money was put out to work, and how is it coming back home to the investor? Reported profit plus depreciation is both a convenient and an accurate way to express this result.

3. *Tax depreciation.* The added cash flow from extra depreciation taken only for tax purposes is a debatable component of an ROI. The mechanics were shown in Chart 2-4. What do you believe? Does an accelerated method truly portray economic reality, or is the straight-line technique often used concurrently for reporting to shareholders a better representation? Take your choice. In this book, the conclusion has been that the more rapid basis is preferable for ROI purposes because it is real in terms of cash results. But there are arguments on the other side, too. Each time the key question emerges: Is this particular cash flow a true reward or isn't it?

4. *Flowthrough of investment credit.* The story is the same as for tax depreciation: another choice. The author's decision has been to show resulting cash flow as a component of return.

5. *Amortization of goodwill, capitalized R&D, patents, and so on.* More choices. In fact, room for another book. This one, being addressed to the executive and not to the technician, places emphasis on the *concept* of reward rather than trying to serve as an encyclopedia of specifics.

Before leaving the definition of return, a few more words. The term "cash flow" used so often in this text implies that all profits are in cash and that certain other inflows of funds should be added to the profit number. Usually the expression is appropriate, but for some companies, reported earnings are not at all synonymous with cash. For example, accounting rules for land developers state that a sale may be recorded once the papers have been signed and a certain percentage of the contract paid. The profit on such a sale is not simultaneously available in cash. Rather, it becomes part of a long-term receivable. For ROI purposes, however, logic dictates that the transaction profit be considered as cash, and the subsequent long-term reloaning to the purchaser a separate matter. Other noncash profits can be viewed similarly. If it's called "profit," somebody believes money was made—and that's a return.

Finally, a reminder that an underlying premise of the ROI calculated for a total business is that results for the individual period being measured are typical. By definition, ROI must encompass the total investment life; but operating statements are published annually. The mental process for understanding this is the same as that for a constant payment plan on a mortgage. If this year's cash flows are to represent the payment rate, calculating the corresponding return is just a matter of arithmetic.

This subject, too, was touched on earlier, but is important enough to amplify. While a "return" can include several components of cash flow, profit and depreciation usually provide the dominant numbers. And the contribution to cash flow from depreciation is directly dependent on the capital intensity of the business being measured. The point to be made is that one cannot properly compare the cash flows of businesses which are dissimilar in their investment requirements.

To see why, look at two companies of the same size but with different investment profiles, as shown in Chart 9-1. Since Company A uses only current assets, the $100, or 10%, cash flow gives a true ROI of 10% (like interest on a savings account). Company B shows a much greater cash flow–more than $2\frac{1}{2}$ times as much–but the ROI still is 10% (refer to Chart 5-8; akin to amortizing a five-year mortgage on a constant payment plan of 26% of the original amount each year).

So the ROI is the same for both companies, but their cash-flow patterns are entirely different.

So the ROI is the same for both companies, but their cash-flow patterns are entirely different.

The repetition above is not a typographical error. The statement is repeated as a way of emphasizing its importance. Notice, too, that a measure of profit alone, or a percentage of profit to assets, gives yet another answer. The fellow with the better "cash flow to

CHART 9-1. Results of two businesses with dissimilar investment requirements.

Company A			
Net working capital[a]	$1,000	Equity	$1,000
Gross fixed assets	—		
Results of operations:			
Profit			$100
Depreciation			—
Total cash flow			$100
% cash flow to gross assets			10%
ROI			10%

Company B			
Net working capital[a]	—	Equity	$1,000
Gross fixed assets	$1,000		
Results of operations:			
Profit			$ 64
Depreciation (5-year life)			200
Total cash flow			$264
% cash flow to gross assets			26.4%
ROI			10%

[a]Current assets minus current liabilities.

83

assets" has the lower "profit to assets." No wonder management can be confused. It reminds one of the popular television program in which a panel is supposed to determine which of three persons alleging to be a specific individual is, in fact, telling the truth. We hear the plea: "Will the true measure of economic accomplishment please stand up!"

There are some interpretive aspects worth mentioning in connection with the previous illustration. The profit reported by Company B is what remains after a charge for depreciation has been deducted. Using 50% as a tax rate, pretax profit would have been $128 and pretax profit before depreciation would have been $328, compared to an amount of $200 for A. So what? Well, if Company B were an automated version of A (which it probably isn't), the savings from installation of capital equipment did in fact lower the costs of production. The company with a heavy capital investment usually will also have low out-of-pocket costs and relatively high fixed, or continuing, costs—which makes profit sensitive to volume fluctuations.

The illustration also compared operating results to initial investment rather than to a year-end balance. The latter portion of Chapter 8 dealt with the matter of reinvestment of cash flows, and Appendix E contains additional technical comments. For most readers, it is sufficient to say that Company B's cash flow included a return of principal as well as "interest," and the principal portion is assumed to be subsequently reinvested to maintain the business at the same level.

In a few words: Companies with big cash flows in relation to assets aren't automatically better than those with smaller cash flows. It depends on how much of the cash flow comes from a recapture of previous capital investments. The outfit with heavy capital requirements is obliged to use a good chunk of its cash flow just to maintain its facilities—it isn't "free" money. ROI puts all this into proper perspective.

Effect of Debt Financing on ROI

There is none. On earnings per share—yes; but on ROI—no! The way a business is financed has absolutely no effect on its true underlying ROI. Nor should it have.

Let's analyze the situation. Chart 9-2 shows two businesses, identical except for the method of financing. For simplicity, the entire investment is employed as working capital.

The leverage associated with debt financing has, of itself, increased reported earnings per share from $1.00 to $1.40. The profit pie is a little smaller with debt because interest must be paid. But in this illustration the number of shares decreased by a greater amount, and the smaller number of shares divided into profits after debt service produced higher earnings per share.

We shall not expound on the pros and cons of different debt/equity ratios. Certainly long-term debt has a role to play in our industrial society. But one must remember that the street is two-way. When times are good, profits per share receive a "kicker" from the infusion of debt; when the trend is reversed, the slide downward is just as rapid.

Earnings per share, by definition, is an expression of the stockholders' stake. But ROI is a function of the business itself, independently of how it is put together. That, too, is by definition. So in order to calculate a proper ROI, effects of various financing methods must be excluded.

All of this is not very complicated or profound. But it is surprising how often it's overlooked. Earnings per share seems to be a determinant of stock prices, and the most

CHART 9-2. Profile of two companies identical except for source of capital.

Company A			
Net working capital	$1,000	Debt	—
		Equity (100 shares)	$1,000

Results of operations:

Profit	$100
% cash flow to investment	10%
ROI	10%
Number of shares	100
Earnings per share	$1.00

Company B			
Net working capital	$1,000	Debt (8%)	$ 400
		Equity (60 shares)	600
		Total	$1,000

Results of operations:

Profit	$ 84
(Pretax debt cost = $32; after tax, $16.)	
% cash flow to investment	10%
(Adjusted to exclude debt.)	
ROI	10%
Number of shares	60
Earnings per share	$1.40

frequently quoted measure of performance. But a topic more basic than the ostensible well-being of the shareholder is the innate performance of the company itself. If the corporate house is built on sand, any illusion of sanguinity associated with a favorable trend in earnings per share ultimately will be shattered. Incurrence of debt for the short-range purpose of boosting earnings per share is nothing less than irresponsible deception. Chapter 11 has more to say about current trends associated with this subject.

Relation Between Changes in Cash Flow and Changes in ROI

If you've ever been strapped for cash and attempted to ease the pain of making payments on a long-term commitment by stretching out the time period, this section will be easy to understand.

Consider a $50,000 mortgage on your new home. The friendly bank officer says that for a 20-year loan at 8% the annual payment will be $5,100. (See Chart 5-8, which tells that 10.2% of the principal must be paid each year to amortize such a debt.) But $5,100 is too much money. How about spreading the payments over 30 years? A pause while the banker flips to another page in his big book full of figures. A weak smile. The annual payment only drops to $4,450 (8.9% repayment rate; see Chart 5-8). So, for an increase of 50% in the time of the loan, the tradeoff is a reduction of 13% in your payments! And truth-in-lending obliges the bank to tell you that the total amount paid on the 20-year basis will be $102,000, while the cash paid out on the 30-year proposition will add to $133,500. On the same amount of debt, you must pay an extra $31,500 for the privilege of "saving" $650 per year in payments during the first 20.

Carrying the illustration to an extreme, a 50-year payment plan would permit further reduction in the annual payment to $4,100, just $350 less than that for 30 years. And for 100 years, the number would be a very few dollars less. The payment rate can never fall below $4,000, because that amount is required to cover annual interest alone on the $50,000 at 8%. Anything above is applied to the principal, which doesn't go down very fast unless payments are substantially above $4,000.

ROI for a business works in exactly the same manner. It's important to recognize this, because changes in cash flow do not affect the return in direct proportion. If results are good to start with, further improvements in cash flow and ROI are roughly parallel. But if cash flows are declining, ROI will drop like a stone. The reason simply is that a certain floor of cash is required just to maintain a repayment of the principal; repayments cannot fall below that level without going into the red from an ROI viewpoint.

Chart 9-3 shows how it looks on a graph. The illustration is the inverse of that for amortizing a mortgage. In the latter case, payments are first applied to a predetermined calculation of interest, with the balance going to the principal. With ROI, the "interest" is determined by measuring how much is available over and above required principal payments. When cash-flow rates aren't sufficient to recoup the initial investment, the result obviously is less than zero.

The thing to remember is that ROIs in the range of, say, 1 to 6% are tenuous; just a little drop-off in cash flow spells trouble. On the other hand, cash flows producing ROIs of 10% or more can change by greater amounts without dramatically impacting the return.

Effect on Profit of Inventory Fluctuations

The following discussion is related only indirectly to ROI but is included under a "while we're at it" rationale. Many executives do not seem to understand how changes in the inventory levels of finished goods influence profits. If ROIs are to be believed and used, behavior patterns of the components of ROI must also be familiar. Here is another dial to be read.

During periods of inventory buildup, reported profits tend to be greater than if inventories were constant. Similarly, during periods of inventory reduction, profits will be less than normal. The degree of effect depends on the importance of fixed, or continuing, costs in the manufacturing operation. And the phenomenon applies primarily to finished goods and work-in-process accounts.

Quite often these outcomes are extremely frustrating to management. A business gets into trouble because sales dipped and nobody turned off the faucet back at the factory (perhaps profits looked okay during this period). Finally things got out of hand. Then a shake-up took place and a new regime was brought in to straighten out the mess. Production was slashed to get inventories back into balance. But the bottom line didn't change all that much. Topside pressure became relentless. The new management was convinced real progress was being made, but the figures didn't show it. Nobody understood why. Patience began to wear thin on both sides.

CHART 9–3. Relationship between cash flow and ROI for investment in depreciable facilities with ten-year life.

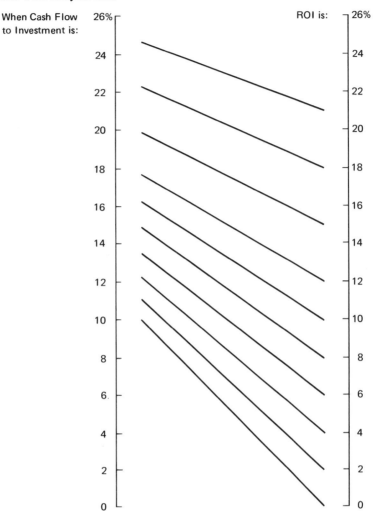

In a situation like this, things might work out in the long run and they might not. Additional decisions prompted by the outward lack of improvement might undercut true gains that were already achieved but not evident. It's tough enough to make money without these problems. So let's try to clear the air and show what really is happening.

An illustration is the easiest way—an example rudimentary enough to display cause and effect in an understandable manner. Assume you own a little paper clip business and utilize a standard cost system which was (properly) developed as follows:

CHART 9–4. Standard cost development for paper clip.

Cost of paper clip wire: 25¢ per M clips
Owner's salary: $200 per month
Normal activity: 400M units per month
Therefore, fixed salary cost per M clips is 50¢
Total standard cost: 25¢ + 50¢ = 75¢
Selling price: $1.00 per M clips

Since the hub of the upcoming problem relates to the valuation of inventories at standard cost, a few words about this may be helpful. In a large corporation, standard costs of some kind are virtually essential as a control device. While they may contain some theoretical deficiencies for inventory-valuation purposes, the pros and cons usually shake out to permit their use on the balance sheet; only when standards are not approximately representative of average manufacturing conditions must an adjustment be made. Because inventory revaluations can be both arbitrary and painful in terms of clerical work and judgmental factors, it's highly desirable to keep the standards up to date and utilitarian.

Let's go on. In the first month of operation, the paper clip business sold exactly what it manufactured. See Chart 9-5. No problem. Results reflect the innate profitability of the business.

CHART 9-5. First month's operation: All production sold.

Sales ($1.00 per M)		$400
Less inventory value (at standard cost) of goods sold:		
Variable (400M units × 25¢)	$100	
Fixed (400M units × 50¢)	200	
		300
Gross margin		$100
Plus manufacturing cost variance		—
Net before tax		$100
% net before tax		25%
First month on cash basis:		
Sales		$400
Less: Wire bought and paid for	$100	
Actual salary	200	
		300
Increase to cash		$100

But the second month is another story. Though customers canceled some of their orders, the factory continued to produce, and even increased output. See Chart 9-6. Notice what happened to profits. In spite of lower sales, income actually increased—both in absolute dollars and as a percentage. A close study of the chart will show why. In essence, the finger points to an overrecovery of overhead normalized for the standard cost development. The activity level adopted in the standard wasn't necessarily wrong; fluctuations obviously occur from month to month—this was just one of them. But because standard rather than actual costs were used for inventory valuation, any variances between the two had to be accounted for somewhere in order to make the books balance. Since this variance did not find a home on the balance sheet, the only place left was the income statement. During the second month the number was "favorable," a reflection of higher-than-normal production, so reported profits benefited. (If actual rather than standard costs had been used for valuing this month's production, and inventories had been kept on a "first-in, first-out" basis, actual costs of $325 would have been spread over the 500M units produced, making each worth 65¢ per M rather than 75¢ per M. With 200M units left in inventory at month-end, their balance-sheet value on this basis would be $130. Inventories are an asset—they're worth something. If one says they are worth more or less than before, the difference must be charged or credited to profit.)

CHART 9-6. Second month's operation: Made 500M units, sold 300M, put balance of 200M into inventory.

Sales ($1.00 per M)		$300
Less inventory value (at standard cost) of goods sold:		
Variable (300M units × 25¢)	$ 75	
Fixed (300M units × 50¢)	150	
		225
Gross margin		$ 75
Manufacturing cost variance (volume gain due to over-recovery of fixed cost by making 500M units rather than 400M—extra 100M units times 50¢ per M)		50
Net before tax		$125
% net before tax		42%
Second month on cash basis:		
Sales		$300
Less: Wire bought and paid for	$125	
Actual salary	200	
		325
Decrease to cash		($ 25)

Now move on to the third month. Production was cut back to reduce the amount of cash tied up in inventory; sales have recovered, but reported profits declined sharply. See Chart 9-7. Though the business certainly showed signs of recovery during the third month, the bottom line didn't follow along. Costs held even, wire was purchased at the same price, and the manager's salary remained unchanged. But profits got worse instead of better!

CHART 9-7. Third month's operation: Made 300M units, sold 500M, took balance required for sales from previous inventory.

Sales ($1.00 per M)		$500
Less inventory value (at standard cost) of goods sold:		
Variable (500M units × 25¢)	$125	
Fixed (500M units × 50¢)	250	
		375
Gross margin		125
Manufacturing cost variance (volume loss due to under-recovery of fixed cost by making 300M units rather than 400M—100M units times 50¢ per M)		(50)
Net before tax		$ 75
% net before tax		15%
Third month on cash basis:		
Sales		$500
Less: Wire bought and paid for	$ 75	
Actual salary	200	
		275
Increase to cash		$225

CHART 9-8. Successive balance sheets for paper clip business.

Balance sheet on opening day:

Assets		Equity	
Cash	$1,000	Net worth	$1,000

Balance sheet at end of first month:

Assets		Equity	
Cash	$1,100	Initial net worth	$1,000
		Profit	100
			$1,100

Balance sheet at end of second month:

Assets		Equity	
Cash	$1,075	Initial net worth	$1,000
Finished goods inventory	150	1st month profit	100
(200M units at 75¢)		2nd month profit	125
	$1,225		$1,225

Balance sheet at end of third month:

Assets		Equity	
Cash	$1,300	Initial net worth	$1,000
Inventory	–	1st month profit	100
	$1,300	2nd month profit	125
		3rd month profit	75
			$1,300

This little bit of accounting alchemy fools many people. Once again, where did the profit variances hide during the second and third months? Answer: They were "capitalized" on the balance sheet. To see how, look at Chart 9-8, which portrays balance-sheet data at the outset and for each of the three operating months.

There is nothing wrong with the bookkeeping. That's the way it is. Notice that everything came out even in the long run. However, as the saying goes: "In the long run, you're dead." Management decisions must be well timed—prompt when promptness is called for, and deferred when corrective measures are accomplishing their purpose. The financial arm has an obligation to contribute to solutions rather than be part of the problem.

Summary

Discussion and examples in this chapter obviously do not cover all the bases associated with analyzing the return. They were only examples of the more common variables. The IBM motto "Think" has a place here. And, as mentioned earlier, this is a proper occasion to play the game of "what if." When ROI is not a familiar subject, one does not always mentally translate changing conditions into their impact on ROI results. But because both the basic theory and clerical effort are easy to work with, there is no excuse for laziness in omitting interpretive activities.

10

Analyzing
the Investment

MOST of the discussion in this chapter is about the fixed-asset portion of the balance sheet. That is where the action normally is in terms of analysis requirements.

Importance of Asset Life in Economic Evaluations

When it comes to spending capital money, management must do a complete job of analysis, or else leave itself highly vulnerable to future shocks. Generally the amounts involved are closely scrutinized. "Do we really need a 40-foot flagpole out in front of the new plant; why not 30-foot?" Or, "Isn't there some way to cut construction costs by substituting such and such here, or such and such there?" Occasionally it's the other way: "Let's do the job right this time and not pinch pennies." The return on investment, however company practice dictates it be calculated, also commands consideration, both from proponents of the project and from those empowered to approve it. All this is necessary and proper.

But only rarely is executive attention focused on the third key economic ingredient of an investment proposal—namely, its life. Remember the illustration in a previous chapter—the mortgage amount, the annual payment, and then a key question: For how many years does all this happen? Like a three-legged stool, it's impossible to say which leg is the most important. In combination they perform their function, and if one component is unsound, the other two won't be able to prevent a collapse. So the matter of asset lives is not something to be left to the accountants. True, tax regulations control to some degree the depreciation charge-off procedure used in determining one's tax bill, but it is a serious mistake to assume that asset lives for tax purposes will automatically coincide with the utility period of capital equipment and facilities.

For example, suppose you are thinking about opening an expensive new motel-restaurant out on the edge of town. The building and furnishings might be good for twenty years from a utilitarian standpoint, but economically the story could be quite different. A new bypass expressway is on the drawing board, and the through traffic you had been counting on could disappear five years from now when the ribbon is cut on the new highway. The proposition still might be worthwhile if you can get your money back and then some before the traffic flow dries up. And there still may be a good residual value of the property for other purposes. The accountants will determine what can be done for tax purposes, but management must call the shots on the economic life of the investment. Chart 4-1 in Chapter 4, the format for calculating an ROI, provides for such contingencies. Merely record the depreciation allowable for tax purposes in the appropriate years and assume that the undepreciated balance at the end of Year 5 is washed out by an additional lump-sum write-off in Year 6, net of any cash proceeds expected from the sale of the property at that time. The "Other" column of cash flow was designed for these things. The same treatment applies when purchasing machinery to manufacture a product whose economic life is likely to be less than the physical capability of the equipment, or when the machinery is likely to become obsolete quickly though the product itself may still be viable.

To better grasp the ROI effect of differing asset lives, look at the simplified illustration in Chart 10-1. The postings on this chart were taken from Chart 5-8. Observe the peculiar pattern, which of itself provides guidance. If the debate is whether economic life

CHART 10-1. ROIs associated with a constant annual cash flow for a varying number of years (assuming annual cash flow = 15% of depreciable investment).

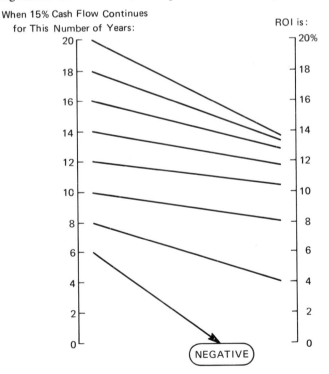

92

should be based on 20 years versus 18 or 16, who cares? The ROI doesn't change much. But at the other end of the scale, if the alternative is between an 8-year and a 10-year life, one had better think it out carefully, because ROI is cut in half (having been marginal to begin with). An infinite number of individual results are possible, depending on how the numbers are put together. For example, can tax depreciation be accelerated if a strong enough case is made for an abnormally short economic life? Does a residual value exist when the project ends? And so on.

Remember that these are economic results. Goodness knows what profit and loss statements will look like during interim years, especially if tax and book depreciation are different and residual values are significant. Chapter 2 described how increased depreciation makes reported profit and cash flow move in opposite directions. The income statement may look terrible, but cash is really flowing! Various tax-shelter investments such as real estate, livestock, and drilling for oil work in exactly this manner, taking advantage of all the law allows in terms of deductions from reported profit. But when it comes to running their own corporations, many executives can't seem to get away from a preoccupation with earnings per share. Chapter 11 will further document this danger. The point being reemphasized here is that conventional accounting sometimes will be more a part of the problem than a contributor to the proper solution. If heavy depreciation charges are taken in early years because of an accelerated basis, almost any project will show a book loss, even though the underlying economics are attractive.

To clearly demonstrate the ROI effect of asset-life variations, discussion and the previous example dealt with a single asset. The same principle applies to a total of depreciable investments. Collectively, are the asset lives appropriate or not? In recent years, some companies have taken a bath by writing off in one year a substantial amount for economic obsolescence of manufacturing facilities. Undoubtedly their hope was that by getting it out of the way at one time, they would avoid many years of dismal earnings reports. Or, to be charitable, perhaps they expected rapid obsolescence because of a recent technological breakthrough. Let others decide. Beyond question, however, is the fact that obsolescence in our technically oriented world is more of a factor today than it was 25 years ago, and in the future probably will be even more significant. Business has recognized this by using ever shorter depreciable lives for its equipment (see Chart 1-2). But this is "on the average." Each company must make sure its own house is in order. Is yours?

There are ways to get a feel for this. Look at an annual report or other published data and note the following:

- The annual rate of depreciation compared to original cost of the assets. Is it 3%, 6%, 9%, or what? Considering the composition of these assets, does this rate seem to mirror the technological climate of the industry?

- The overall percentage by which total fixed assets have been depreciated (i.e., reserve for depreciation divided by original cost). Is it 20%, 40%, 60%, or what? Is the business mature or relatively young and dynamic? How do the competitors look on this basis?

- A capital expenditure history usually is shown somewhere in the report. At what rate has the company been adding or replacing in recent years?

Interpretation becomes a matter of judgment, and presumes some knowledge of the industry. In electronics, for example, one would expect both a high depreciation rate and, unless the company is very new, a substantial percent reserve for depreciation; sizable annual capital expenditures also are likely. In the computer industry, a number of firms are trying to make a living by purchasing equipment and leasing it out at rates lower than those of the OEM. The lower rates are primarily a function of a longer anticipated life, and book depreciation charges reflect this assumption.

So an investor first must ponder the validity of such practices before attempting to evaluate published financial results. One also can gain some valuable insights by comparing a company's asset accounting practices with the practices of others in the same business. To sum up, before dancing to the piper of earnings per share, we want to find out how long the music will last.

<table>
<tr><td>Effects of
Inflation</td><td>

Inflation is a cancer insidiously penetrating and choking the vitals of our (relatively) free enterprise system. Even if inflation is kept under reasonable control in the future, more damage already has been done than most people are aware of or want to think about. Despite a veneer of satisfactory current results, many businesses are in deep trouble, or will be very soon. And the options remaining—even for survival alone—are becoming both few and increasingly restrictive.

It's difficult enough to cope with the short-term effects of inflation—higher food prices today than last month or last year, increases in the cost of clothing, automobiles, raw materials, or other consumables with a relatively short economic life. These symptoms are readily apparent; they make the headlines. Wage rates advance year to year. Costs of producing and marketing go up. Business must seek higher prices in order to protect profit margins. Because the condition is so visible, everybody talks about it, and (hopefully) works on it. And of course they should.

But an even larger problem has been building beneath the surface. It affects those with massive capital investments in long-lived facilities—the companies we know as heavy industry. The replacement cycle here is much longer, perhaps 20 years or more. So an investment now necessary to reproduce this productive capacity is not just 5, 10, or 15% higher than when originally put into use, but for older facilities probably more than double the original cost. And this doesn't consider added capital requirements imposed by today's society—pollution control equipment, zoning regulations, and amenities now common for employee convenience and safety.

Assume you are associated with such a capital-intensive industry. If new capacity is required, either because the old is worn out or to supply increased trade demand, the fellow who first takes the plunge may be in for a difficult time. If product price levels currently reflect a proper return on the old, pre-inflation investment—itself an optimistic assumption—what justification is there to assume higher industrywide prices solely because one producer recently spent a lot of money for a new plant? It just won't happen. So no one may build for a while. Finally, the entire industry is comprised largely of antiquated facilities. Then some dramatic event exposes an incipient shortage of the product and several new plants are built or expanded at approximately the same time. Enough demand, coupled with the fact that now most of the manufacturers must have higher prices to achieve a proper ROI, can lead to a happy ending for all.

But what a tortuous and risky path. The wrong timing will spell disaster. Decisions must consider not only the environment of direct competitors, but that of indirect ones.

</td></tr>
</table>

And the environments of suppliers. Executives earn their salaries wrestling with such basic issues, and an ROI approach will help in sorting out the risks associated with various options.

Unfortunately, the endings aren't always going to be pleasant. Many companies, even many industries, have backed themselves into a terrible corner over the years. Their product prices scarcely provide an adequate ROI on the lower capital investments of years ago. Wooden-headed pricing departments add up costs and tack on a margin for profit, but the "costs" include only the nominal depreciation expense of an old facility (see Chart 2-7). In some cases, management may not even recognize the problem. After all, "profit to net assets" or "profit to total capital"–common pseudo ROI measures–still show up well. Of course they do, based on depreciated values, but Chapter 3 showed why that kind of an answer is deceitful. Try calculating your "normal" prices under the ROI approach in Chapter 7 when using replacement values of capital facilities, and see where you come out. That, in a nutshell, will tell how big the problem is.

Look at it this way. If replacement facilities will cost twice as much and working capital in the business is comparatively insignificant, cash flow also must double to maintain the same ROI. (If your mortgage doubles in size, and the life and interest rate are unchanged, the payments must double.) If you work out the arithmetic, it will show that profit before tax and before depreciation must double, and profit after tax must also double, in order for cash flow to be twice as much. That's a lot of money–not just 10 or 20% more, but double.

Not the least part of the problem is the source of new money for capital replacement. Where will it come from? Certainly not from depreciation of old facilities. Remember, costs have now doubled. Not from profits, unless ROI for the business is well above recent averages for durable goods manufacturers. Not from debt, unless the company is among the minority that has not already used up most of its debt capacity. So that leaves equity financing. And who is going to put new money into a venture under these conditions?

In the March 1, 1971 issue of *Forbes* magazine, an experienced and successful economist by the name of Julian Gumperz indirectly addressed this situation. He said:

> Corporations during the next four or five years are going to be pushed out of the money markets and into the equity markets. The average U.S. industrial corporation today has over a 40% debt-to-equity ratio. That ratio will probably have to come down. But even if they *want* to take on more debt, they are going to be pushed aside in a stampede for long-term borrowing by all levels of government and all types of public utilities.

Mr. Gumperz's comments were related to stock market behavior, not to ROI. But they serve to emphasize the immense capital investments that will be required of U.S. industry in coming years–capital investments that collectively show dim prospects for achieving a satisfactory ROI.

Pity the poor utilities, whose continuing need for new capital is almost insatiable. These companies have their activities and rates controlled by a multitude of governmental bodies (and are subject to all the political pressures associated therewith); are saddled with a rate-base formula that usually has nothing to do with future capital requirements and inflated capital-investment costs; and are experiencing a declining quality of debt because of progressively lower fixed-charge coverage. One must question the prospects for survival of these as privately held corporations. On top of everything else, they and others are paying taxes on profits which are too high because depreciation charges are inadequate to renew and maintain the business. To repeat, where is the money going to come from? We're on a collision course. This is not just an opinion. No other conclusion can be drawn from an analysis of the facts. The only alternative is stagnation. The railroads are already there.

Undervalued Assets

The problems here are similar to those associated with inflation, but the circumstances are a little different and special remarks are in order. Common examples of undervalued assets are natural resources—land, mineral deposits, timber, and the like. These often are carried on a balance sheet at costs prevailing decades ago (in the case of land) or at ridiculously low net-of-depletion amounts (as in the case of wasting assets). Their presence can boost up a company's ROI, since today's profits and cash flows are related to an artificially low asset base. Management, too, may say: "Look at the fine ROI we are earning," without giving serious thought to the unreal basis of the calculation.

More important, the illusion of success obscures fundamentals that might lead to another conclusion. Specifically, are these assets being employed in an optimum manner? What are the alternatives? Maybe more money could be made by selling them off and reinvesting the proceeds. The form used in Chapter 4 can be adapted to answer these questions, or at least the purely financial side of them. For example, if a parcel of land on the books for $10,000 could be sold to a developer at an after-tax profit of $100,000, and the land is now contributing to cash flow only $5,000 per year as a mineral resource, the reasoning must be that in forgoing the $100,000 we save $5,000 annually. Or, to rephrase as a question, would you rather have $100,000 now or an assurance of $5,000 annually for an indefinite period? From an ROI standpoint, the $5,000 annually is equivalent to a 5% return, which is not very much.

A decision of this nature obviously will involve many nonfinancial business judgments. If you sell off the mineral land or whatever, how do you expect to stay in the mining business? Here is the counter: If you're going to stay in the mining business for a while, you'd better be sure that a satisfactory ROI is there based on the true value of the land and other resources employed. Don't kid yourself by using an artificially low asset base that automatically shows a fine return. Maybe, just maybe, a realistic calculation of present and alternative results might become the first step in a strategic decision to phase out that activity, to begin to take profits and run, to search for a new field of endeavor where an investment of the $100,000 proceeds from the above sale might generate much more than the $5,000 cash flow now being recorded. There are emotional deterrents to getting out of a business; sometimes management will not entertain such a thought until forced to. But an ROI approach may be able to express the issue in a way that stimulates the thinking process.

Notice from the preceding discussion that ROI comes into play in selling as well as in buying. The essence of the matter on the selling side is what is going to happen to money realized from a sale. What are the alternatives? The cash must be put to use again; the task is to choose the best outlet.

As mentioned previously, this is not a textbook on accounting practice. Depreciation methods, acquisitions, and a variety of business transactions can be recorded in different acceptable ways. The important thing is to understand what has been done. Then one can reach one's own conclusions on whether to accept the numbers as shown or to recast them into another format.

The capitalizing of certain costs such as research expense, goodwill, and interest on construction has an effect on the ROI as calculated in this book. We shall take a little space to show why and how. Let's use research as the example. Since most companies capitalizing R&D will do so only for book purposes and will at the same time claim the deduction as an expense for tax purposes, we shall follow that route. Chart 10–2

CHART 10–2. Effect on ROI of amortizing research.

	Year 1	Year 2 and Thereafter
Company A (Research Expensed)		
Net earnings before research	$ 500M	$ 500M
Less research	100M	—
Net earnings before tax	$ 400M	$ 500M
Less tax (@ 50%)	200M	250M
Net profit	$ 200M	$ 250M
Assets:		
Plant and equipment	$1,000M	$1,000M
Annual cash flow to assets	20%	25%
Estimated life	10 years	10 years
ROI	15.1%	21.4%
Company B ($100M Research Amortized Over 5 Years)	*Year 1*	*Year 2*
Net earnings before research	$ 500M	$ 500M
Less research amortization	20M	20M
Net earnings before tax	$ 480M	$ 480M
Less current tax (@ 50%)	200M	250M
Less deferred tax	40M	(10M)
Net profit	$ 240M	$ 240M
Total cash flow (as used for ROI)	$ 240M	$ 240M
Assets:		
Plant and equipment	$1,000M	$1,000M
Net research (treated as current asset)	80M	60M
Total assets	$1,080M	$1,060M
Annual cash flow to assets	22.2%	22.6%
Estimated life	10 years	10 years
ROI	18.2%	18.6%

compares the results for two companies with different practices. At issue is $100,000 of research expense in Year 1. Company A expenses this one-time cost, while Company B capitalizes it as an asset and depreciates the "investment" over five years.

By expensing this one-time cost, Company A has reduced its Year 1 ROI to 15.1%; the return then recovered to 21.4% for Year 2 and thereafter. Company B, by capitalizing, added to both its asset base and its reported earnings; the transaction improved ROI in Year 1 (versus expensing), though in future years the return was lower than for Company A as the amortization ran its course. Simply stated, capitalizing leveled out both profit and the ROI effect of a presumably unique and long-lasting research effort.

The ROI mechanics leave room for discussion. In the example, cash flow does not include either amortization or the deferred tax. The logic, as explained in Chapter 8, is that capitalized research expense in an annual report is always shown "net," not gross less an amount amortized to date; mathematical integrity for ROI requires that under these conditions it be treated as a current asset, and that cash flows exclude the effects of amortization. Theoretically, the preference would be to treat both investment and cash flow in a manner identical to that for other depreciable assets, but the absence of available starting data rules this out. Fortunately, under either approach the practical difference usually is nominal. More could be said, but additional messages would be directed to the analyst, not to the executive for whom this book is intended.

Off-Balance-Sheet Financing

Off-balance-sheet financing refers to assets employed in connection with a certain type of long-term lease. Under this particular arrangement, nothing is shown on the balance sheet either to recognize the value of the asset itself or to indicate a long-term contractual liability associated with its use. So far as ROI is concerned, the answer is: "Yes, these should be capitalized."

This would be a good place to stop, because discussion of balance-sheet recording for leases can quickly become complex. Proper accounting has been debated for many years, and some issues still are not settled. For example, how a specific transaction is structured for statement purposes depends on the basic intentions of the lessor and lessee, detailed terms and payments, life of the asset (assuming in fact a true asset is involved rather than a contract for service), existence of options to renew or purchase, probable residual value at the end of the contract period, presence or absence of an arm's-length relationship between lessor and lessee, rights of each party, and so on. Different accounting treatments are permitted or prescribed for varying combinations of the above.

If a long-term lease already is recognized in some manner on the balance sheet, one usually is best advised to follow along and accept the treatment shown. To do otherwise requires a rather thorough knowledge of the inner workings of accounting for this specialized subject, something most people don't have. As noted previously, accounting and economics may have different objectives; separate them where you can. For example, capitalized amounts sometimes are shown at "discounted" values—a complication for an ROI approach which is oriented to original investment.

Our concern at this time is to recognize leases which, for technical reasons only, have not been capitalized in some manner. Except to an insider, complete information to do this with precision probably isn't available, so one has to take a stab at it. Footnotes to financial statements provide the best hunting ground for clues, which usually are in the form of a listing of annual payment obligations. With this as the only data to work with, one must impute a capitalized value. For general-purpose buildings with useful lives in the range of 20 years and up, a rule-of-thumb amount of ten times the annual lease payment is suggested. Such a figure would normally provide to the lessor a reasonable return under relatively modest conditions of risk. It's impossible to be more specific because circumstances will vary. Chart 10-3 shows the mechanics.

Pause for a minute. Why all the fuss—carried to the extreme of guestimating new numbers to plug into a balance sheet? The answer, repeated for emphasis several times in this book, is that the innate return for a business must be separated from the sources of its financing. These are separate subjects, just as sales dollars and cost dollars are different matters. They are related; sometimes they influence each other. But merely knowing the spread between the two is not, of itself, enough information to manage a business properly.

See what happened in Chart 10-3. The ROI dropped from 15.0% to 10.8% after the long-term lease was capitalized. Why? Because we now have in one place all of the investment—regardless of who made it—and all of the return. Look at it this way. You're out in Las Vegas playing the slots. You borrow a dollar from your wife and feed the machine. Up come three bells and eighteen dollars fall out. What was your ROI? A first reaction might be to say "infinity." You didn't put a cent of your own money out to risk, but received $18.00 and used $1.00 to repay your wife. So what was your wife's return?

CHART 10-3. How to capitalize a lease for ROI purposes when using ten times annual lease payment as capitalized amount.

	Annual Report Basis	Capitalization of Lease Adjustments	Adjusted Basis for ROI
Income Statement:			
Sales	$100,000		$100,000
Less costs (excluding lease payment)	75,000		75,000
Less building lease expense	5,500	(5,500)	—
Less depreciation	—	2,750[a]	2,750
Pretax profit	$ 19,500		$ 22,250
Tax @ 50%	9,750		11,125
Net profit	$ 9,750		$ 11,125
Cash Flow:			
Net profit	$ 9,750		$ 11,125
Depreciation	—	2,750	2,750
Total	$ 9,750		$ 13,875
Balance Sheet:			
Net current assets	$ 65,000		$ 65,000
Gross fixed assets	—	55,000[b]	$ 55,000
Investment	$ 65,000		$120,000
Average life	—		20 years
ROI	15.0%		10.8%

[a] Twenty years; straight-line depreciation.
[b] Lease payment × 10.

Nothing, really, under this way of thinking. She loaned you a dollar and you paid her back the dollar. But the true return for the transaction itself was in the relation of $18.00 of reward to $1.00 of investment. Similarly, the ROI in Chart 10-3 is reduced to 10.8% when all of the capital employed is related to all of the reward.

The above principle often comes into play when ROIs are determined for individual investment proposals. Someone comes along and says: "Let me have $65,000 and I'll get you a 15% ROI." But as Chart 10-3 shows, a lease commitment is involved, and the true ROI on the project itself is only 10.8% when the full $120,000 investment is considered. It works this way because the lessor is satisfied with a lower return than is projected on the total transaction. Regardless of how the numbers are put together, it's obvious that in order to be in the black, enough must be earned to pay the lessor an amount sufficient to amortize his principal plus his return.

This discussion is in no way a condemnation of leasing. Often the practice makes good business sense. The point, repeated once again, is to separate the true return for the business from the influence of its financing. Banks and credit companies can react comparatively quickly to changes in the spread between the cost of funds and the return earned from lending, but most manufacturing businesses cannot. Commitments of the latter are more permanent from every standpoint.

Valuation of Current Assets

Most of the time this portion of the investment is "clean" in terms of valuation, but it's worthwhile to take a quick look at things which can cause trouble.

Inventory-valuation techniques influence balance-sheet amounts. An extremely low-cost LIFO base, for example, has the effect of both lowering current earnings and reducing the stated investment. Or standard costs may be some distance from reality—though probably not too far, or an adjustment would be required by public accountants. The current value of investments made long ago in other companies might be quite different from the book cost. In these instances, the comments of a few pages back about undervalued assets also would apply here.

Summary

The objective of the past two chapters has been to stimulate the reader's thinking. The listing of a group of figures in a precise and orderly manner, and their "certification" as proper balance-sheet and profit and loss reports, doesn't guarantee their correctness in an economic sense. Accounting has its job to do; but so does economics. An executive must first recognize that there is a difference. Managing a business on the basis of published numbers does not necessarily insure success. But managing it on a sound basis economically does insure that satisfactory published results will follow. The next chapter takes us around the last lap and attempts to drive this point home.

11

Analyzing
the Trend

A POPULAR TV commercial features the comment: "Sooner or later, we're gonna getcha." Normally such negative advertising might repel rather than attract, but in this case it apparently sells the product.

The relationship of earnings per share and ROI trends can be stated either negatively or positively, either as a threat or a promise:

- When year-to-year ROI trends are downward, there is no power of accounting, economics, or logic that can prevent an ultimate decline in EPS.

- When ROI trends are upward, earnings per share will bask in ROI's reflection and make life pleasant for management and stockholders.

The important thing to recognize is that ROI leads and EPS follows, rather than the other way around.

Choose your own orientation. View these statements as "sounding the alarm," or view them as a new opportunity to foretell and thus better manage the long-term health of your business. But regard them you must, because they are as fundamental as sunrise and sunset or the ebb and flow of the tides. Numerous references to this precept were made in previous chapters. Now let's confirm these assertions.

**Example Involving
Current Assets
Only and No Debt**

The following examples are simplified. A ten-year sequence of events is divided, for convenience, into three successive periods of four, three, and three years each. Assume first that only current assets are involved—it's easier to understand that way. (A later example will deal with fixed assets.) Mentally acknowledge that the numbers compress into relatively few years a trend of results which may take fifteen or twenty years, or even longer. These are the ground rules:

- An initial investment in current assets of $1,000.
- A sales-to-asset ratio of 1.5 to 1 (current-year sales to beginning assets).
- All profits are reinvested—no dividends.
- Capitalization of 100 shares of stock—no debt initially.
- A declining ROI pattern: 15% the first year, 14% the second year, 13% the third, and so on.

Chart 11-1 gives the results for Years 1 through 4. Let's study it for a bit. Many of the figures shown are derived; they are the result of other numbers which led the way, numbers dictated by the ground rules. Look at Year 3. The key calculation around which other results pivot is the 13% ROI for that year. Thirteen percent of the $1,311 investment at the beginning of the year is $170, so $170 is also the cash flow, the profit, and the amount reinvested in the business. Sales and costs are backed into. Sales of $1,967 are merely one and a half times the beginning assets. Since profit after tax is established at $170, pretax profit is twice as much, and "all costs" is the difference. Percent profit to sales and earnings per share also fall into place. Not all of the statistics are essential to the calculation; they are intended to provide a frame for the picture.

The example is "rigged" only in the sense that ROI is destined to fall by one point per year. Everything else is logical.

CHART 11-1. First four years' results under declining ROI pattern with increasing earnings-per-share trend (current assets).

	Year 1 Beginning	Year 1 End	Year 2 End	Year 3 End	Year 4 End
Sales		$1,500	$1,725	$1,967	$2,222
Less all costs		1,200	1,403	1,627	1,866
Pretax profit		$ 300	$ 322	$ 340	$ 356
Tax @ 50%		150	161	170	178
Net after tax		$ 150	$ 161	$ 170	$ 178
% profit to sales		10.0%	9.3%	8.6%	8.0%
Earnings per share (100 shares)		$ 1.50	$ 1.61	$ 1.70	$ 1.78
Cash reinvested		$ 150	$ 161	$ 170	$ 178
Current assets	$1,000	$1,150	$1,311	$1,481	$1,659
Equity	1,000	1,150	1,311	1,481	1,659
ROI		15%	14%	13%	12%
Cash flow required to attain predetermined ROI		$ 150	$ 161	$ 170	$ 178

NOTE: In this example, ROI for a year is calculated on the assets invested at the beginning of a year (i.e., at the end of the previous year). Thus, first-year cash flow required to earn a 15% ROI is 15% of the initial investment of $1,000; for the second year, a 14% ROI is earned on the beginning balance of $1,150, so 14% of $1,150 is $161, and so on. Remember: When only current assets are involved, the profit *is* the ROI, just like interest on a savings account in which the principal remains intact.

Now forget for a minute everything about ROI and concentrate on earnings per share. While the ROI analyst is beginning to "view with alarm," management may be "pointing with pride." The annual report for the fourth year might well read as follows:

> We are pleased to report our third consecutive year of sales improvement. This year's shipments increased by $255, an amount greater than the gain of $242 enjoyed in the prior year. More important, earnings per share also rose again—to $1.78—and maintained the consistent upward trend of previous years. Shareholder equity is now $1,659, a 66% increase from the $1,000 initial capitalization.

The security analysts consult their computers. Here is an outfit going places—for three years in a row both sales and earnings are up. Flash the "buy" signal. But the company is starting to go downhill. EPS is up simply because of a higher asset base. If you put $100 in the bank and earn 6%, or $6.00, the first year, the new balance is $106. Next year the bank may pay only $5\frac{3}{4}$%, but your annual earnings increase to $6.095, a higher absolute amount. This is only because the investment base is bigger. So long as the amount on deposit grows enough to more than offset a decline in interest rate, the absolute dollars of interest keep inching upward. In stripped-down fashion, that's all there is to it. Not very profound or complicated, but so often overshadowed by a preoccupation with EPS.

The trend of improvement in EPS cannot continue indefinitely while ROI continues to decline. Chart 11-2 shows the next three years in the life of this company. Year 7 is the turning point. The asset base has continued to grow, but a persistent lowering of the rate of return finally reduced the absolute reward to a number below that for the previous year. The reasons could be many. Perhaps the original investment still is earning at a 15%

CHART 11-2. Fifth through seventh years' results under declining ROI pattern.

	Year 5 Beginning	Year 5 End	Year 6 End	Year 7 End
Sales		$2,489	$2,762	$3,038
All costs		2,125	2,394	2,674
Pretax profit		$ 364	$ 368	$ 364
Tax (@ 50%)		182	184	182
Net after tax		$ 182	$ 184	$ 182
% profit to sales		7.3%	6.7%	6.0%
Earnings per share (100 shares)		$ 1.82	$ 1.84	$ 1.82
Cash reinvested		$ 182	$ 184	$ 182
Current assets	$1,659	$1,841	$2,025	$2,207
Equity	1.659	1,841	2,025	2,207
ROI[a]		11%	10%	9%
Cash flow required to attain predetermined ROI		$ 182	$ 184	$ 182

[a]Based on beginning-of-year assets; e.g., 10% is on $1,841 to get $184.

ROI, but reinvested funds have not generated much of a reward. Or the entire base could be eroding. The end result is the same. Nevertheless, an annual report for Year 7 might still exude optimism. After all, business is a rocky road and progress is uneven. The chairman is addressing the shareholders:

> Over the six full years of your company's existence, sales have increased in each and every year. Though the increase this past year was a little less than for the prior year, we are pleased with the consistent upward trend. Earnings per share, though slightly below that of last year, were nevertheless the second highest in our history. Shareholder equity at year-end again increased significantly, and is now $2,207 compared to $1,000 when the company was born. We are confident that next year will show . . . etc., etc.

But the ROI for Year 7 was down to 9%, a full 40% below the 15% figure of Year 1. From here on things begin to fall apart. The trend is continued in Chart 11-3.

The value of this information to management should now be obvious. ROI not only provides a concept on which a system of total financial management can be based, but also both foretells and governs the future trend of earnings per share.

Please reread the preceding sentence. It is one of the most important in this book.

There is no direct relationship between the topping out of EPS in Year 6 and the 9% ROI in Year 7. A 9% ROI is not necessarily a crossover point. If ROI were declining more gradually, EPS might continue to rise even after ROI had eroded to as low as the 5% level. The rate of ROI decline is the control. Once more, the thing to remember is that eventually EPS must follow.

CHART 11-3. Eighth through tenth years' results under declining ROI pattern.

	Year 8 Beginning	Year 8 End	Year 9 End	Year 10 End
Sales		$3,311	$3,576	$3,827
All costs		2,957	3,242	3,521
Pretax profit		$ 354	$ 334	$ 306
Tax (@ 50%)		177	167	153
Net after tax		$ 177	$ 167	$ 153
% profit to sales		5.3%	4.7%	4.0%
Earnings per share (100 shares)		$ 1.77	$ 1.67	$ 1.53
Cash reinvested		$ 177	$ 167	$ 153
Current assets	$2,207	$2,384	$2,551	$2,704
Equity	2,207	2,384	2,551	2,704
ROI[a]		8%	7%	6%
Cash flow required to attain predetermined ROI		$ 177	$ 167	$ 153

[a]Based on beginning-of-year assets; e.g., 7% is on $2,384 to equal $167.

By taking on long-term debt, management can postpone for a while the inevitable falloff in EPS associated with a deteriorating ROI trend. It's the same as in everyday life. A person may buy a new car he really can't afford. After making the monthly payment, there isn't enough left over for groceries. A trip to the local finance company provides cash needed now. Meanwhile, the neighbors wonder at the display of affluence. Sooner or later, however, the moment of truth will come. And the crisis then will be more traumatic because an illusion of well-being is suddenly shattered—and everyone will know it. The same thing can happen in the corporate world.

Chart 11-4 picks up from the previous series of illustrations. Now, however, "your company has elected to take advantage of new opportunities" by "utilizing our untapped resource of debt capacity."

The sarcasm is not at all intended as a general indictment of debt itself, but is used to emphasize that management (and shareholders) must have a way of knowing when debt is being used as a cover-up for deteriorating performance. The years from 7 on are reworked to show the addition of this debt. Compare the EPSs in this chart with those in Charts 11-2 and 11-3. What a difference. Though ROI results are the same, debt has acted

CHART 11-4. ROI in seventh through ninth years when results are modified to recognize incurrence of debt.

	Year 7 Beginning	Year 7 End	Year 8 Beginning	Year 8 End	Year 9 Beginning	Year 9 End
Sales		$3,337		$3,929		$4,749
Less all costs except interest		2,937		3,511		4,304
Less interest (@ 6%)		12		24		45
Pretax profit		$ 388		$ 394		$ 400
Tax @ 50%		194		197		200
Net after tax		$ 194		$ 197		$ 200
% profit to sales		5.8%		5.0%		4.2%
Earnings per share (100 shares)		$ 1.94		$ 1.97		$ 2.00
Cash reinvested		$ 194		$ 197		$ 200
Current assets	$2,225	$2,419	$2,619	$2,816	$3,166	$3,366
New long-term debt incurred at start of year (6%)	200		200		350	
Total year-end debt		200		400		750
Equity	$2,025	$2,219	$2,219	$2,416	$2,416	$2,616
ROI[a]		9%		8%		7%
Cash flow required to attain predetermined ROI		$ 200		$ 209		$ 222

[a]Based on beginning-of-year assets and based on true business performance independently of financing method. Thus, interest has after-tax effect on earnings of $6.00. To say it another way, in year 7 business really earned $200 and used $6.00 (after tax) to pay interest on source of funds.

as a "kicker" to reported profits. The reason is plain. Any profits earned on debt money in excess of its interest cost flow to the shareholders. They're getting a return on somebody else's investment.

Each time new debt is pumped in, it provides a stimulus to EPS. But the doses have to be larger and larger if all this happens while ROI is going down. Notice that the first $200 of debt in Year 7 boosted EPS to $1.94 compared with the $1.82 result excluding debt, a 12¢ gain. But the $350 of debt added in Year 9 was not enough money power to make big year-to-year progress in the face of a continuing erosion of ROI. The hill is getting steeper.

Chart 11–5 continues the example to the hilltop and down the other side. Year 10 is the last year new borrowing can be incurred. The bankers are beginning to make noises because debt is now about one-third of total capitalization. So EPS is no longer stimulated. In Years 11 and 12 the inevitable begins to occur—a very sharp falloff in profits. Observe that the decline is now much steeper than in the illustration without debt. Effects of the adrenaline have worn off and the corporate body is debilitated. This company has painted itself into a corner, and no maneuvering room is left. Even if the year-to-year decline in ROI were now arrested, irreparable damage may have been done.

CHART 11–5. ROI in tenth through twelfth years, recognizing existence of debt.

	Year 10 Beginning	Year 10 End	Year 11 End	Year 12 End
Sales		$6,099	$6,400	$6,655
Less all costs except interest		5,610	5,973	6,300
Less interest (@ 6%)		87	87	87
Pretax profit		$ 402	$ 340	$ 268
Tax @ 50%		201	170	134
Net after tax		$ 201	$ 170	$ 134
% profit to sales		3.3%	2.7%	2.0%
Earnings per share (100 shares)		$ 2.01	$ 1.70	$ 1.34
Cash reinvested		$ 201	$ 170	$ 134
Current assets	$4,066	$4,267	$4,437	$4,571
New long-term debt incurred at start of year (6%)	700			
Total year-end debt		1,450	1,450	1,450
Equity	$2,616	$2,817	$2,987	$3,121
ROI[a]		6%	5%	4%
Cash flow required to attain predetermined ROI		$ 244	$ 213	$ 177

[a]Based on beginning-of-year assets.

Let's see what happens if, in Year 11 and following, the ROI were to level off at 6%. Chart 11–6 records it.

CHART 11–6. ROI in eleventh through thirteenth year continuing at 6%.

	Year 11 Beginning	Year 11 End	Year 12 End	Year 13 End
Sales		$6,400	$6,720	$7,059
Less all costs except interest		5,887	6,181	6,494
Less interest (@ 6%)		87	87	87
Pretax profit		$ 426	$ 452	$ 478
Tax @ 50%		213	226	239
Net after tax		$ 213	$ 226	$ 239
% profit to sales		3.3%	3.4%	3.4%
Earnings per share (100 shares)		$ 2.13	$ 2.26	$ 2.39
Cash reinvested		$ 213	$ 226	$ 239
Current assets	$4,267	$4,480	$4,706	$4,945
Debt	1,450	1,450	1,450	1,450
Equity	$2,817	$3,030	$3,256	$3,495
ROI[a]		6%	6%	6%
Cash flow required to maintain predetermined ROI		$ 256	$ 269	$ 282

[a]Based on beginning-of-year assets.

When ROI holds constant, EPS will begin to rise again. Such is true whether ROI levels off at 1% or 10%. The company is earning a positive return, and on the surface the record is impressive. EPS has increased without interruption every year since inception, as shown in Chart 11–7, which traces the chronology.

CHART 11–7. Earnings-per-share record of company in example.

Year	EPS	Year	EPS
1	$1.50	8	$1.97
2	1.61	9	2.00
3	1.70	10	2.01
4	1.78	11	2.13
5	1.82	12	2.26
6	1.84	13	2.39
7	1.94		

The situation portrayed in Chart 11-7 approximates that of many industrial corporations today. The only difference is that the time span in this example is compressed into about half that of average real-world experience.

So what's the matter with these results? Nothing—if you are satisfied with perilous stagnation. Though a veneer still shines, the structure has developed serious weaknesses. A low absolute ROI indicates a precarious existence, because only a small additional decline in cash flow means big trouble (Chart 9-3). This company almost certainly is no longer a leader in its field. It's unlikely to be the low-cost producer. It has joined the ranks of the living dead. "Survival of the fittest" is an axiom also applicable to the business world, and debilitation increases the odds for further decline rather than for a spontaneous revival. In a few words, the company is highly vulnerable to either total failure or a dramatic shake-up. These statements are not made with reference to the leveling of ROI, but rather are pointed to the low absolute number associated with its stabilization.

Here is the bind. The company cannot take on much more debt because the capitalization structure already has used up borrowing capacity. And a stock issue also is unlikely, because the issuing price necessary to prevent a dilution in EPS very probably is higher than the present market price. In other words, it will be extremely difficult to get any more new money to take advantage of true opportunities and get things moving again; the chance for real progress is thus defaulted to others, and the net draws tighter. The only course left is "operation bootstrap," a long and painful process.

Chart 11-8 describes the problem, picking up the action in Chart 11-6 with Year 14. Illustrated are two trials involving a stock issue, one at a multiple of 12 times previous year's earnings, and another at 15 times. Neither provides enough funds to prevent a decline in EPS, simply because new money earning only a 6% ROI is not rewarding enough to prevent a dilution in EPS.

It's a matter of arithmetic. New stock must be issued at a price in excess of 16 times previous year's earnings in order for EPS to go up. By the time management recognizes impact of a low ROI, it may be too late for the stock to command such a price. The exact numbers in this particular illustration are clouded somewhat by the presence of debt, but the fundamentals are easily recognized. If ROI were up in the 10% range, stock could be issued at 10 times earnings without reducing EPS (assuming continuation of the same ROI). But if ROI is, for example, at 2%, stock must be issued at 50 times earnings to maintain EPS (again assuming continuation at the 2% rate). In other words, with a good ROI people will be standing in line to put in more money and the stock probably will carry a high multiple because a good ROI also will produce a rapidly climbing pattern of EPS. But if the reverse is true, the stock will be trading at a low multiple and new funds at that price will depress EPS.

What about book value, which at the end of Year 13 was $34.95 per share (Chart 11-6; $3,495 equity divided by 100 shares)? Yes, what about it? It was explained earlier that book value as a stand-alone statistic means little. Assets must be related to earning power. The previous charts witness to that fact. Book value is rising year by year, but earnings aren't keeping pace. Sooner or later the stock price will fall below book. An ROI approach tells the whole story; book value provides only a hint.

The discussion above is basic. For emphasis, and to make sure the message gets across, the key point will be repeated in paraphrase. Suppose a company is earning $2.00 per share but the ROI is only 6%. For simplicity, all the assets are current and amount to

CHART 11–8. EPS results in Year 14 when new stock is issued.

	Year 14		Year 14	
	Beginning	End	Beginning	End
Sales		$11,719		$12,795
Less all costs except interest		10,780		11,772
Less interest (@ 6%)		87		87
Pretax profit		$ 852		$ 936
Tax @ 50%		426		468
Net after tax		$ 426		$ 468
% profit to sales		3.6%		3.7%
Issue another 100 shares:				
@ 12 × prior-year EPS of $2.39	$2,868			
@ 15 × prior-year EPS of $2.39			$3,585	
Earnings per share (200 shares)		$ 2.13		$ 2.34
Cash reinvested		$ 426		$ 468
Current assets	$7,813	$ 8,239	$8,530	$ 8,998
Debt	1,450	1,450	1,450	1,450
Equity	$6,363	$ 6,789	$7,080	$ 7,548
ROI[a]		6%		6%
Cash flow required to maintain predetermined ROI		$ 469		$ 511

[a]Based on beginning-of-year assets.

$1,000,000, so a 6% ROI on $1,000,000 is $60,000. Thirty thousand shares are outstanding. Recognizing that stock prices fluctuate widely, an average historical multiple for such a company might be about 15, so the stock will trade around $30. A new issue of 10,000 shares at $30 will bring in $300,000. If the company is capable of earning only a 6% ROI, these new funds will generate an additional $18,000 in profit. Therefore, total earnings will rise to $78,000 ($60,000 plus $18,000) for the 40,000 shares and EPS will drop from $2.00 to $1.95.

See what would happen if the ROI above were down to 4%. Again use $1,000,000 in current assets. Profit is $40,000, 30,000 shares are out, EPS is $1.33, and the price multiple is 15; so the stock trades at $20. Ten thousand new shares are issued at $20; the proceeds of $200,000 also earn 4%, or $8,000. Now total earnings are $48,000 for 40,000 shares, or $1.20 versus $1.33 before the new issue. At a 4% ROI, only if new stock can be issued at 25 times earnings ($33.33) does enough new money ($333,333) come in so that combined EPS on new and old stock is maintained at $1.33. New funds of $333,333 then are added to existing capital of $1,000,000 for a total of $1,333,333, and a 4% return is $53,333. Dividing return by 40,000 outstanding shares yields $1.33; thus the original earnings rate is maintained. But who is going to pay 25 times earnings for this kind of performance? It just doesn't fit together.

If the basic ROI were 10%, the picture would be entirely different. On $1,000,000 in current assets, profit is $100,000; 30,000 shares are out; EPS is $3.33; and a price multiple of 15 is again assumed. The stock thus trades at $50. Ten thousand new shares are issued for $500,000, and $50,000 is earned on the new money. So new total earnings of $150,000 divided by new total shares of 40,000 gives an EPS of $3.75, a number higher than that earned originally.

Now maybe the actual stock-price multiple will be 10 or 20 or whatever. The point is that the poorer the ROI, the higher the issue price required on new stock in order to maintain existing EPS—and vice versa. But the real world moves in the opposite direction. A leveling off of results will tend to depress rather than stimulate the stock price. This is why a company in this position is handcuffed in its efforts to raise new money to "get things moving forward again." Bear in mind that the previous calculations are illustrative— they apply exactly only when all assets are current. Different numbers will go with different combinations of fixed and current; emphasis here is on the principle and the trend.

What if new money really will, in fact, improve overall ROI? Well and good. But a management whose track record has been poor will need a convincing story to get its ideas financed. By the time a low ROI is evident, it may be too late to do more than try to work out of it as best one can.

To repeat, the sequence reviewed above is becoming the profile of more and more industrial corporations. The tragedy is not only that this happens, but that the trend and the underlying reasons continue unrecognized. There still is time for corrective measures, but not much. The more deterioration, the more difficult it will be to turn things around. Some big companies won't make it unless their trend reverses very soon.

Example of ROI and EPS Trends Using Fixed Assets Only

The previous illustrations worked with current assets because the calculation is a little easier to understand. For fixed assets the pattern is similar, and to complete the story, a "clean" example will be shown. The ground rules are:

- An initial investment in fixed assets of $1,000.
- Straight-line depreciation over 20 years.
- All profits reinvested—no dividends.
- A sales-to-asset ratio of 1.5 to 1 (current-year sales to beginning assets).
- Capitalization of 100 shares of stock—no debt initially.
- A declining ROI pattern: 15% the first year, 14% the second year, and so on.

Chart 11-9 shows the results for the first four years. Annual cash flows required are greater than in Chart 11-1, where only current assets were involved. This is because the repayment includes amortization of the initial investment, a depreciable asset. The proceeds are immediately reinvested in additional fixed assets, which builds the base. Once again, the first four years show good EPS progress in the face of a declining ROI. However, Chart 11-10 shows that during the next four years the picture changes and a persistent decline in ROI begins to pull down EPS.

There is no need to continue with succeeding years. Enough evidence has been given. The numbers follow the same pattern as that for current assets. Here, too, new debt can

CHART 11-9. First four years' results under declining ROI pattern with increasing earnings-per-share trend (fixed assets).

	Year 1 Beginning	Year 1 End	Year 2 End	Year 3 End	Year 4 End
Sales		$1,500	$1,740	$2,003	$2,289
Less all costs except depreciation		1,230	1,448	1,688	1,957
Less depreciation (20-year life)		50	58	67	76
Pretax profit		$ 220	$ 234	$ 248	$ 256
Tax @ 50%		110	117	124	128
Net after tax		$ 110	$ 117	$ 124	$ 128
% profit to sales		7.3%	6.7%	6.2%	5.6%
Earnings per share (100 shares)		$ 1.10	$ 1.17	$ 1.24	$ 1.28
Cash flow per share		1.60	1.75	1.91	2.04
Cash reinvested		$ 160	$ 175	$ 191	$ 204
Gross fixed assets	$1,000	$1,160	$1,335	$1,526	$1,730
Reserve for depreciation		50	108	175	251
Net fixed assets		1,110	1,227	1,351	1,479
Equity	$1,000	$1,110	$1,227	$1,351	$1,479
ROI		15%	14%	13%	12%
Cash-flow dollars to attain predetermined ROI		$ 160	$ 175	$ 191	$ 204
Cash-flow percent to attain predetermined ROI (Chart 5-8)		16.0%	15.1%	14.3%	13.4%

NOTE: In this example, ROI for a year is calculated on the gross assets invested at the beginning of a year (i.e., at the end of the previous year). Thus, first-year cash flow required to earn a 15% ROI is 16% of the initial investment of $1,000; for the second year, a 14% ROI is earned on the beginning balance of $1,160, requiring a 15.1% cash flow on $1,160, or $175; and so on.

mask a declining ROI by temporarily revitalizing EPS—and here, too, a collapse is inevitable if ROI does not recover or at least stabilize. Issuance of new stock becomes increasingly difficult as ROI declines and more assets are needed to maintain EPS; the multiple required to avoid dilution rises to an unreal number.

Though most businesses utilize a combination of current and fixed assets, results were analyzed separately for ease in understanding.

A Closer Look

In the interest of getting the message across, the previous illustrations and related comments spotlighted the basic ROI-versus-EPS issue. There is more to be learned from a review of trends.

Perhaps the reader noticed that the statistic of "percent profit to sales" also declined each year as ROI went down. Is there a correlation? Can ROI trends be inferred from a review of profit-margin trends?

CHART 11-10. Second four years' results under declining ROI pattern (fixed assets).

	Year 5 Beginning	Year 5 End	Year 6 End	Year 7 End	Year 8 End
Sales		$2,595	$2,922	$3,264	$3,623
Less all costs except depreciation		2,246	2,563	2,895	3,252
Less depreciation (20-year life)		87	97	109	121
Pretax profit		$ 262	$ 262	$ 260	$ 250
Tax @ 50%		131	131	130	125
Net after tax		$ 131	$ 131	$ 130	$ 125
% profit to sales		5.0%	4.5%	4.0%	3.5%
Earnings per share (100 shares)		$ 1.31	$ 1.31	$ 1.30	$ 1.25
Cash flow per share		2.18	2.28	2.39	2.46
Cash reinvested		$ 218	$ 228	$ 239	$ 246
Gross fixed assets	$1,730	$1,948	$2,176	$2,415	$2,661
Reserve for depreciation	251	338	435	544	665
Net fixed assets	1,479	1,610	1,741	1,871	1,996
Equity	$1,479	$1,610	$1,741	$1,871	$1,996
ROI[a]		11%	10%	9%	8%
Cash-flow dollars to attain predetermined ROI		$ 218	$ 228	$ 239	$ 246
Cash-flow percent to attain predetermined ROI (Chart 5–8)		12.6%	11.7%	11.0%	10.2%

[a]Based on beginning-of-year assets.

Not precisely. The parallel existed only because the ground rules froze the sales-to-gross-assets ratio at 1.5 to 1. Appendix A shows that over the past 25 years more and more assets have been required to generate a dollar of sales. Expressed another way, sales have not risen as fast as assets, and profit margins in the real world therefore have not declined as much as they would have if the relationship were frozen.

Chart 11-11 recaps the "percent profit to sales" figures from Charts 11-9 and 11-10. It also shows what these are when the sales-to-gross-assets ratio declines steadily during the eight years from 1.50 to 1.15, a change roughly parallel to that experienced by durable goods manufacturers over the past 25 years.

The decline in profit margins is not erased, but is blunted considerably. The purpose of reviewing this phenomenon is to again remind percent-to-sales worshippers to pay heed to the asset power required to generate both volume and profit. Actually, ROI can be falling even without a decline in percent to sales, though such occasions probably are exceptional. Usually a decline in percent to sales is a warning sign indicating deterioration in ROI.

Another condition temporarily influencing the trend of ROI arises from a delay in putting new assets to work. When additional financing—debt or equity—is for major expansion, it takes time to purchase or construct new facilities, so they can't be expected to generate a return on day 1. Study and interpretation is needed. Is a change in ROI

CHART 11-11. Percent profit to sales from Charts 11-9 and 11-10 compared to percent profit to sales under a declining sales/asset ratio.

Year	% Profit to Sales Under Constant 1.5 to 1 Sales/Asset Ratio	Revised Sales/Asset Ratio	Recalculated % Profit to Sales Using Revised Sales/Asset Ratio
1	7.3%	1.50	7.3%
2	6.7	1.45	7.0
3	6.2	1.40	6.6
4	5.6	1.35	6.2
5	5.0	1.30	5.8
6	4.5	1.25	5.4
7	4.0	1.20	5.0
8	3.5	1.15	4.5

NOTE: Sales/asset ratios in Charts 11-9 and 11-10 based on sales to beginning-of-year gross assets.

caused primarily by these circumstances, or are poor results being covered up by such an explanation? A review of longer-term trends should provide guidance.

Other crosscurrents also come into play. There is the corporate dividend policy, for example. To the extent that dividends are paid, the compounding effect of earnings is watered down. There is nothing inherently good or bad about it, it's just another thing to monitor. Use of accelerated depreciation also affects results, and analysis is made more difficult when different bases are used for book and tax reporting. Management can be fooled by an illusion of prosperity associated with a good cash flow stimulated by fast depreciation write-offs, and overlook the fact that such money is necessary for replacement of worn-out or obsolete facilities. Even worse, a company may be paying dividends from these funds now, and then have to borrow money later to keep up the same dividend rate because internally generated cash is not sufficient to both renew facilities and compensate the shareholders.

Conventional approaches to financial analysis don't reveal the trends discussed in this chapter. We have seen how incomplete and even misleading P&L and balance-sheet data can be. The first step in solving a problem—or diagnosing an illness—is to recognize it exists. ROI gets to the heart of the matter. The corporate body, like the human body, can exhibit a variety of symptoms either of health or of sickness. If treatment is called for, it must be the illness that is dealt with, not just the symptoms. ROI points the way. Continuing in a philosophical vein, this is a good place to say again that we have been addressing financial issues which are a product, not the cause, of management actions. Winning or losing may be reflected in the numbers, but it was the combination of all prior business decisions that produced these numbers in the first place. Better facts and better diagnoses will improve the odds for success.

A final comment about trends. Alvin Toffler's book *Future Shock** describes how the roaring current of change is accelerating everywhere in our society. The personal and sociological implications alone are as much frightening as they are challenging, and the business world is an integral part of this phenomenon. Changes that used to span a century now are being compressed into perhaps a decade, and all signs point to an even faster pace in the future. Evolution is becoming revolution. Manufactured products have

*New York: Random House, 1970.

a shorter life span; ingredients used in making them are discarded and replaced more quickly, as is the manufacturing process itself; and equipment and facilities, which used to be good for 20, 30, or 40 years, are now becoming obsolescent or worn out in a fraction of that time. This is particularly important to a capital-intensive business. Management will have to be even faster on its feet. Trend analyses of all kinds, not only ROI, will inevitably play a more important role in the future. There simply won't be time to react after the fact.

Summary

The thrust of this chapter may be summed up in very few words. Corporate progress traditionally has been measured with an earnings-per-share yardstick. But ROI is really the governing influence—the cause and not the result. Thus, future trends in EPS are made both more predictable and more manageable by strategic planning based on an ROI orientation.

Previous chapters emphasized first a proper definition of ROI; next, its qualifications as a relevant and precise financial measure of business results. Then followed discussion of the versatility of ROI—its application to a wide variety of business decisions. Now we have completed the final segment, the compass ROI provides to steer the future course of a business.

12

Observations
and Reflections

THIS brief final chapter is one of meditation—with a little preaching interspersed. Also included are a few thoughts which didn't seem to fit anywhere else.

Reacting to the Alarm Bell

Where do we stand on the subject of ROI? More important, where are we going? The keynote message of this book warns that American industry is headed for trouble because its financial underpinnings are being eroded. How should a reader react to this unpleasant prophecy? Does it parallel doomsday predictions of coastal California slipping into the Pacific Ocean? If the allegations are true, why isn't the subject getting more attention?

An average businessman doesn't have the time or resources to pursue these questions. Instead, further study and organized efforts to confirm, publicize, and correct the alarming trend probably will have to originate in the universities and in professional organizations serving management. It had better begin soon.

What Do I Do Now?

But the average executive is involved too, because his own fortunes are inexorably linked to his company's return on investment. The first step is to see and believe that conventional financial yardsticks are in fact incomplete and can be misleading, or both. This will be the biggest obstacle for many. "Who needs ROI? We're doing OK without adding another way to keep score." But are you really? If no other section of the book was motivating, Chapter 11 by itself should provide convincing evidence that earnings per share is the follower and ROI is the leader. Prove it to yourself. It really isn't much work to calculate your own corporate ROI trend over the past several years and chart the pattern alongside EPS. Use the convenient form in Appendix D. (Not the least of the benefits will come from forced attention to the matter of asset life. How vulnerable is the capital-investment base to economic obsolescence?) If your results are typical, you'll be shocked—and ROI will move from a casual-reading file to an immediate-action folder.

Converting to an ROI orientation will be no small task for some. Habits and experience of many years are going to be upset. The change in approach will spotlight undesirable conditions previously obscured, and may point an accusing finger at activities formerly looked on with favor. Questions will be many, and time will be needed to "break in" the new way of life as it pervades all corners of the business. Meanwhile, the detailed sequence of organizing and implementing this effort is vulnerable to inertia and delay. Thorough advance preparation and education is a must.

Nowadays most corporations motivate and reward key executives through some form of supplementary incentive compensation. There is no better way to inaugurate an ROI philosophy than to incorporate it in a management bonus plan. Then any doubts are removed. Executives up and down the line know the scorekeeping rules, and are impelled to manage their respective areas accordingly.

Perhaps a few may overreact and expect ROI to solve all their financial problems. That's not right either. Conventional accounting reports—income and expense statements, funds-flow analyses, and balance sheets—are here to stay. They are primarily tactical reports. ROI is strategic. Comparisons of this month's ROI with last month's are improper. ROI is directional, not a day-to-day measure. The secret of success lies in harmonizing and integrating ROI into a total format of financial management.

The Negative Side of ROI

A few people have taken a deprecating attitude toward ROI, so it's appropriate to spend a few moments looking at the other view. Detractors seem to emphasize three points. First, ROI is said to be weak because it doesn't fit in with "transfer pricing" among units of a single company. Transfer pricing is of itself a complicated subject. Should various overheads be included or not? Who gets the profit? And so on. However, it's difficult to understand how or why ROI should bear any criticism. On the contrary, it will be more a help than a hindrance in transfer pricing because of a better identification of profit with investment; in other words, regardless of the transfer technique adopted, the effect will be more easily understood when it is ROI-related. Transfer pricing, as a highly specialized subject, might produce under extreme circumstances a few instances where ROI does not contribute to knowledge or direction. But such exceptions if and where they exist are no justification for discarding the overwhelming majority of useful applications.

A second alleged negative is that ROI emphasizes the investment, and many line managers have no responsibility in this area; their job is to make a profit. This reasoning demonstrates a common misunderstanding. As noted a few paragraphs earlier, ROI is a strategic rather than a short-term measure. The shop foreman doesn't need to be a financial expert; his job is to get today's work out today, and he is measured by his cost and effectiveness in doing so. That's the way it should be. The plant manager, however, usually has broader responsibilities for the overall welfare and direction of the business. Therefore, his motivation might include ROI as well as a profit goal. In other words, to whatever organizational level an obligation for business planning is delegated, a responsibility for ROI should follow in the same degree. If it isn't that way now—change it!

Finally, ROI is said to be deficient because it discourages capital spending for modernization and instead encourages "milking the franchise." An offsetting argument can be used: Without an ROI approach, managers don't care what they spend for new assets so long as profit dollars go up. Both extremes are invalid. Incisive analyses will show up attempts to look good today at the expense of tomorrow. Restraint on capital spending may turn out to be proper if the long-term future of the plant (or process, or product) is cloudy. A competent management also will recognize, as many do now, that some capital expenditures do not produce immediate results either on the P&L statement or from an ROI viewpoint. If there is a criticism, it is better directed at actions of management than at the financial techniques for evaluating the results of those actions.

After reading this book, some might suggest a fourth reservation. Though the theory advocated may be pure and true, a number of practical applications require a fair amount of judgmental intervention. For example, the ROI for durable goods manufacturers in 1972 is listed as 7.36% (Appendix A). The calculation is based on an ostensible composite of asset lives, and on the assumption that cash flows and assets for that year are typical; different assumptions would produce different answers. Sometimes even the mathematics invoke decisions which, for convenience, are arbitrary—that cash flows apply proportionally to fixed and current assets, for example. These conditions are admitted without apology; the task of refinement is not finished. Sometimes, however, the need to stop and think at decision points in the calculation is a mirror of important options involving the business itself. Then conscious management involvement is both necessary and appropriate. Finally, ROI like accounting may be scientific in theory, but will remain largely an art form in practice. Specific ground rules will evolve as usage dictates.

The Time-Bomb
Aspect
of Inflation

The impact of inflation on capital-intensive industries was discussed earlier, but it's important enough to emphasize again. Keynesian philosophy, which suggests a little inflation isn't so bad, seems to have become part of our way of life. Most attention is directed toward keeping the rate within bounds, and day-to-day headlines deal primarily with fresh developments and their near-term impact. As both sales and profits continue to rise, business results may appear on the surface to remain satisfactory. Overlooked or ignored, however, is the fact that current performance is based on capital outlays made at the lower costs of years ago. Worse yet, some popular measures of well-being—return on net assets, for example—tend to be improved by the declining value of the dollar. Over a period of time, the compounding of even modest annual inflation rates has added to a sizable figure. The cumulative effect is hidden so long as an existing capital investment continues to produce, but what will happen to profits and ROI when obsolescence or wear and tear makes a new investment mandatory?

It's not a pleasant thing to think about, but this tomorrow will surely arrive. Equally important, where is the capital going to come from to finance the massive outlays required by today's higher prices? Certainly not from today's profits. Stock? Debt? With many companies already in a capital bind, the attraction for potential lenders and investors will not be sufficient to elicit the necessary funds. Then what? The outlook isn't at all encouraging. ROI by itself won't erase the problem, but can provide guidance in coping with it.

Toward a Consensus

Current business commentary seems almost unmindful of the true fundamentals of ROI or the need and opportunity it is capable of serving. Professional journals occasionally contain brief ROI-oriented articles, but most often these are narrowly confined to such topics as capital budgeting techniques, or offer complex mathematical approaches directed toward specific problems. When trends are analyzed by financial magazines and newspapers, it is profit or cash flow that usually forms the theme. When evaluations are made, it is return on equity or book value or some other title at the head of the column.

Yet there seems to be a sense of uneasiness, an underlying awareness that the focus is being directed to effects rather than causes, to pieces instead of the whole. The words "return on . . ." are appearing more frequently, even though the object of attention may be inadequate as a base and interpretation of the result may be more convenient than precise. The first step toward a consensus must come from understanding, and this book was written in the hope of making such a contribution.

Appendixes

	1947	1948	1949	1950	1951
Current assets	$ 27,031	$ 31,062	$ 30,738	$ 38,580	$ 44,982
"Other" assets	2,773	3,295	3,048	3,344	4,001
Less: Current liabilities	9,678	11,598	9,970	15,663	21,344
Net current and "other" assets	$ 20,126	$ 22,759	$ 23,816	$ 26,261	$ 27,639
Plus: Gross fixed assets	23,175	30,147	31,680	33,947	39,433
Investment*	$ 43,301	$ 52,906	$ 55,496	$ 60,208	$ 67,072
Debt other than current	$ 3,554	$ 5,441	$ 5,157	$ 4,912	$ 6,305
Equity	29,318	33,899	36,083	40,020	43,022
Capitalization*	$ 32,872	$ 39,340	$ 41,240	$ 44,932	$ 49,327
Net after-tax profits	$ 4,200	$ 5,386	$ 4,470	$ 6,719	$ 5,665
Plus: Book depreciation	1,252	1,392	1,500	1,672	1,915
Cash flow	$ 5,452	$ 6,778	$ 5,970	$ 8,391	$ 7,580
Plus: After-tax interest on long-term debt (3%)*	107	163	155	147	189
Adjusted cash flow*	$ 5,559	$ 6,941	$ 6,125	$ 8,538	$ 7,769
Percent profit/equity*	14.3	15.9	12.4	16.8	13.2
Percent cash flow/equity*	18.60	19.99	16.55	20.97	17.62
Percent cash flow (adjusted)/investment*	12.84	13.12	11.04	14.18	11.58
Percent debt/capitalization*	10.8	13.8	12.5	10.9	12.8
Percent return on investment*	11.89	12.55	10.19	13.68	10.71
Annual depreciation rate*	5.40	4.62	4.73	4.93	4.86
Sales	$ 70,603	$ 75,254	$ 70,296	$ 86,796	$102,631
Percent net profit to sales*	5.95	7.16	6.36	7.74	5.52
Sales $ per $ of investment*	1.63	1.42	1.27	1.44	1.53

	1960	1961	1962	1963	1964
Current assets	$ 74,879	$ 75,808	$ 81,825	$ 87,814	$ 93,928
"Other" assets	9,574	10,168	11,221	11,764	12,034
Less: Current liabilities	31,122	30,614	33,642	36,347	39,616
Net current and "other" assets	$ 53,331	$ 55,362	$ 59,404	$ 63,231	$ 66,346
Plus: Gross fixed assets	87,307	93,875	99,628	105,435	113,142
Investment*	$140,638	$149,237	$159,032	$168,666	$179,448
Debt other than current	$ 16,338	$ 18,343	$ 19,883	$ 21,163	$ 22,379
Equity	82,262	84,868	89,138	93,340	98,639
Capitalization*	$ 98,600	$103,211	$109,021	$114,503	$121,018
Net after-tax profits	$ 7,032	$ 6,858	$ 8,564	$ 9,471	$ 11,600
Plus: Book depreciation	5,206	5,592	6,206	6,618	7,156
Cash flow	$ 12,238	$ 12,450	$ 14,770	$ 16,089	$ 18,756
Plus: After-tax interest on long-term debt (3%)*	490	550	596	635	671
Adjusted cash flow*	$ 12,728	$ 13,000	$ 15,366	$ 16,724	$ 19,427
Percent profit/equity*	8.5	8.1	9.6	10.1	11.8
Percent cash flow/equity*	14.9	14.7	16.6	17.2	19.0
Percent cash flow (adjusted)/investment*	9.05	8.71	9.66	9.92	10.83
Percent debt/capitalization*	16.6	17.8	18.2	18.5	18.5
Percent return on investment*	6.76	6.27	7.32	7.60	8.73
Annual depreciation rate*	5.96	5.96	6.23	6.28	6.32
Sales	$173,892	$175,207	$195,320	$209,037	$226,297
Percent net profit to sales*	4.04	3.91	4.39	4.53	5.13
Sales $ per $ of investment*	1.24	1.17	1.23	1.24	1.48

DATA SOURCE: Federal Trade Commission, *Quarterly Financial Report*. Items marked by asterisk were calculated or estimated by author.

Statistical Data and Selected Measures of Performance, 1947–1972 (Billions of $).

1952	1953	1954	1955	1956	1957	1958	1959
$ 54,956	$ 53,721	$ 52,851	$ 60,310	$ 65,805	$ 67,005	$ 63,621	$ 70,944
4,314	4,502	4,717	5,062	6,229	6,843	7,292	8,439
24,910	25,393	23,097	26,925	30,103	29,240	25,458	29,033
$ 34,360	$ 32,830	$ 34,471	$ 38,447	$ 41,931	$ 44,608	$ 45,455	$ 50,350
46,996	50,827	54,828	58,088	66,590	74,245	76,611	81,009
$ 81,356	$ 83,657	$ 89,299	$ 96,535	$108,521	$118,853	$122,066	$131,359
$ 9,974	$ 7,918	$ 8,607	$ 9,327	$ 11,771	$ 13,349	$ 14,036	$ 14,954
50,548	53,076	55,818	60,319	66,726	72,172	72,794	77,942
$ 60,522	$ 60,994	$ 64,425	$ 69,646	$ 78,497	$ 85,521	$ 86,830	$ 92,896
$ 5,511	$ 5,804	$ 5,642	$ 8,089	$ 8,335	$ 7,941	$ 5,805	$ 8,067
2,470	2,941	3,267	3,654	4,137	4,545	4,728	4,893
$ 7,981	$ 8,745	$ 8,909	$ 11,743	$ 12,472	$ 12,486	$ 10,533	$ 12,960
299	238	258	280	353	400	421	449
$ 8,280	$ 8,983	$ 9,167	$ 12,023	$ 12,825	$ 12,886	$ 10,954	$ 13,409
10.9	10.9	10.1	13.4	12.5	11.0	8.0	10.4
15.79	16.48	15.96	19.47	18.69	17.30	14.5	16.6
10.18	10.74	10.27	12.45	11.82	10.84	8.97	10.21
16.5	13.0	13.4	13.4	15.0	15.6	16.2	16.1
8.86	9.10	8.37	10.87	10.09	8.92	6.42	8.23
5.26	5.79	5.96	6.29	6.21	6.12	6.17	6.04
$122,316	$137,912	$121,748	$142,088	$159,484	$165,968	$149,626	$169,284
4.51	4.21	4.63	5.69	5.23	4.78	3.88	4.77
1.50	1.65	1.36	1.47	1.47	1.40	1.23	1.29

1965	1966	1967	1968	1969	1970	1971	1972
$103,307	$115,942	$125,328	$138,821	$153,910	$161,287	$165,411	$181,752
12,926	14,292	16,459	19,686	25,284	30,328	33,565	35,022
45,504	53,545	58,022	65,052	76,255	83,412	84,204	90,756
$ 70,729	$ 76,689	$ 83,765	$ 93,455	$102,939	$108,203	$114,772	$126,018
123,586	137,716	154,081	171,006	188,214	205,314	217,390	229,992
$194,316	$214,405	$237,846	$264,461	$291,153	$313,517	$332,162	$356,010
$ 25,858	$ 30,707	$ 37,313	$ 45,455	$ 52,798	$ 60,276	$ 66,332	$ 71,048
105,370	115,169	124,991	135,633	147,563	155,097	160,578	171,908
$131,228	$145,876	$162,304	$181,088	$200,361	$215,373	$226,910	$242,956
$ 14,538	$ 16,372	$ 14,579	$ 16,522	$ 16,875	$ 12,883	$ 14,504	$ 18,441
7,841	8,898	10,153	11,065	11,903	12,781	13,747	15,829
$ 22,379	$ 25,270	$ 24,732	$ 27,587	$ 28,778	$ 25,664	$ 28,251	$ 34,270
776	921	1,119	1,364	1,584	1,808	1,990	2,131
$ 23,155	$ 26,191	$ 25,851	$ 28,951	$ 30,362	$ 27,472	$ 30,241	$ 36,401
13.8	14.2	11.7	12.2	11.4	8.3	9.0	10.7
21.2	21.9	19.8	20.3	19.5	16.5	17.6	19.9
11.92	12.22	10.87	10.95	10.43	8.76	9.10	10.22
19.7	21.1	23.0	25.1	26.4	28.0	29.2	29.2
10.09	10.35	8.52	8.73	8.16	5.99	6.33	7.36
6.34	6.46	6.59	6.47	6.32	6.23	6.32	6.88
$256,951	$291,865	$300,646	$335,497	$366,478	$363,104	$381,598	$436,020
5.66	5.61	4.85	4.92	4.60	3.55	3.80	4.23
1.32	1.36	1.26	1.27	1.26	1.16	1.15	1.22

Appendix B (to Chapter 5): Technical Discussion of Minor Mathematical Flaw in Composite ROI Calculation

The recommended technique for calculating a composite ROI for a number of separate but unidentifiable investment and cash-flow combinations (total-business ROI) contains a minor mathematical inaccuracy.

A simple example of $100 in current assets and $300 in gross fixed assets was used to construct Chart B-1. The actual cash flows required to obtain true returns on investment of 5%, 10%, and 15% over lives of 5 years, 10 years, and 15 years were determined using compound interest and annuity tables. Using these cash flows, returns on the $400 investment were calculated by the composite technique and are shown in the body of the chart. As can be seen, the inaccuracy becomes significant only in situations where the investment has a short average life and/or low return.

CHART B-1. Composite ROI as calculated compared to true ROI.

True ROI	Composite ROI		
	5-Year Life	10-Year Life	15-Year Life
5%	3.73%	3.79%	4.38%
10	7.98	9.34	9.75
15	13.48	14.62	14.90

To understand the problem and one alternative technique, two points should be remembered:

1. The ROI is synonymous with the annual rate of interest being paid on the amount of the total outstanding investment.
2. The cash flow not only pays the interest but, in the case of wasting assets, recovers the principal over the total life.

Since an investment in net current assets is totally recoverable at some future date, on this portion of the investment the cash flow must pay only interest. But on wasting assets, cash flow is applicable to both principal and interest. Herein lies the problem.

Weighting the annual return on the total investment to determine the current portion of the composite ROI assumes that interest is being paid at that annual rate on the net current assets. Conversely, looking up the value of the same annual return in the amortization table assumes that a lower rate of interest is being paid on the wasting portion of the investment, because only part of the payment covers interest—the rest is principal. This can never be, as both types of assets are part of a total corporate entity, earning one cash flow and one rate of interest, or ROI.

There is at least one alternative technique which overcomes this problem and improves the accuracy of the composite ROI. Since all assets earn the same rate of interest in a composite approach, and rate of interest is synonymous with ROI, the rate paid on net current assets is the rate for the total business. As the annual rate can be determined by dividing cash flow by investment, it is relatively simple to apportion the total cash flow in such a manner that the amount left over after paying interest on current assets will result in the same interest rate being associated with recovering the principle over the average life of the wasting assets.

Here is an example of the alternative technique. Assume the following:

Net current assets	$ 300	or	30% of total assets
Gross fixed assets	700	or	70% of total assets
Total assets	$1,000		
Average life	5 years		
Cash flow	$200		

We know that more than a proportional share of the total cash flow must be allocated to the wasting assets because of the need to also recover the principal. So, whatever the percent of wasting to total assets, add 10 and assign this new percent of the total cash flow to wasting assets and the remainder to net current assets. See Chart B-2.

CHART B-2. Calculation of composite ROI using alternative method.

First Trial: 20/80% Cash-Flow Allocation

$$\frac{20\% \text{ of cash flow}}{\text{Current assets}} = \frac{\$40}{\$300} = 13.33\%$$

$$\frac{80\% \text{ of cash flow}}{\text{Fixed assets}} = \frac{\$160}{\$700} = .2286$$

Chart 5-8 look-up indicates   4.60%

Second Trial: 10/90% Cash-Flow Allocation

$$\frac{10\% \text{ of cash flow}}{\text{Current assets}} = \frac{\$20}{\$300} = 6.67\%$$

$$\frac{90\% \text{ of cash flow}}{\text{Current assets}} = \frac{\$180}{\$700} = .2571$$

Chart 5-8 look-up indicates   9.00%

Interpolation

	Percent Cash Flow to Current Assets (ROI)	ROI on Gross Fixed Assets (from Amortization Table)		Difference
Trial 1	13.33%	4.60%		8.73%
Trial 2	6.67	9.00		2.33
Difference	6.66%		Total	11.06%

$$\frac{2.33}{11.06} = .2107$$

$$.2107 \times 6.66 = 1.40$$
$$1.40 + 6.67 = 8.07$$

Composite return on investment: 8.07%

In the example, 80% is assigned to fixed and 20% to current. Dividing 20% of the cash flow by the current assets gives 13.33%, which is a first estimate of the composite ROI. Dividing 80% of the cash flow by fixed assets gives an annual rate of 22.86%, which we now look up in the amortization table for 5 years. The interpolated answer is about 4.6% rate of return. Since the estimated composite rate is higher than that indicated for the wasting-asset portion, more than 80% of the cash flow is required to pay interest and principal.

Let's try a 90%/10% allocation. This yields an estimated composite ROI of 6.67% and an indicated return on wasting assets of 9%. Now we have allocated too much to wasting assets, so the true ROI must be between 13.3% and 6.67%. Under simple interpolation the answer is 8.07%.

Project A, Without Working Capital

PROJECT EVALUATION – SINGLE INVESTMENT

INVESTMENT

Year	Annual Period	Capital Facilities	Expensed Items	Working Funds	Total Investment
	0	10,000			10,000

CASH FLOW / CALCULATION OF RATE OF RETURN

Year	Annual Period At End	N.A.T. Profits	Depreciation	Other	Total	Trial 15% Factor	15% Present Value	Trial 30% Factor	30% Present Value	Trial 45% Factor	45% Present Value	Trial 60% Factor	60% Present Value	Trial 75% Factor	75% Present Value
	0					1.000		1.000		1.000		1.000		1.000	
	1st	4,375	5,000		9,375	.870		.769		.690	6,469	.625	5,859	.571	
	2nd	4,375	5,000		9,375	.756		.592		.476	4,463	.391	3,666	.327	
	3rd					.658		.455		.328		.244		.187	
	4th					.572		.350		.226		.153		.107	
	5th					.497		.269		.156		.095		.061	
	6th					.432		.207		.108		.060		.035	
	7th					.376		.159		.074		.037		.020	
	8th					.327		.123		.051		.023		.011	
	9th					.284		.094		.035		.015		.006	
	10th					.247		.073		.024		.009		.004	
	11th														
	12th														
	13th														
	14th														
TOTAL		8,750	10,000		18,750						10,932		9,525		

INTERPOLATION

$$\frac{932}{\text{(Pres. Val. @ Low Rate Minus Investment)}} \div \frac{1,407}{\begin{array}{c}\text{(Pres. Val. @ Low Rate Minus}\\ \text{Pres. Val. @ High Rate)}\end{array}} = .66$$

$$\times \quad \frac{15.0}{\begin{array}{c}\text{(% High Disc. Rate Minus}\\ \text{% Low Disc. Rate)}\end{array}}$$

$$= \quad 9.9$$

$$+ \quad \frac{45.0}{\text{(% Low Disc. Rate)}}$$

$$\underline{\quad 54.9\% \quad} \text{ ROI}$$

Project B, Without Working Capital

PROJECT EVALUATION – SINGLE INVESTMENT

INVESTMENT

Year	Annual Period	Capital Facilities	Expensed Items	Working Funds	Total Investment
	0	12,000			12,000

CASH FLOW / CALCULATION OF RATE OF RETURN

Year	Annual Period At End	N.A.T. Profits	Depreciation	Other	Total	Trial 15% Disc. Rate Factor	Present Value	Trial 30% Disc. Rate Factor	Present Value	Trial 45% Disc. Rate Factor	Present Value	Trial 60% Disc. Rate Factor	Present Value	Trial 75% Disc. Rate Factor	Present Value
	0					1.000		1.000		1.000		1.000		1.000	
	1st	4,500	1,500		6,000	.870		.769		.690	4,140	.625	3,750	.571	
	2nd	4,500	1,500		6,000	.756		.592		.476	2,856	.391	2,346	.327	
	3rd	4,500	1,500		6,000	.658		.455		.328	1,968	.244	1,464	.187	
	4th	4,500	1,500		6,000	.572		.350		.226	1,356	.153	918	.107	
	5th	4,500	1,500		6,000	.497		.269		.156	936	.095	570	.061	
	6th	4,500	1,500		6,000	.432		.207		.108	648	.060	360	.035	
	7th	4,500	1,500		6,000	.376		.159		.074	444	.037	222	.020	
	8th	4,500	1,500		6,000	.327		.123		.051	306	.023	138	.011	
	9th					.284		.094		.035		.015		.006	
	10th					.247		.073		.024		.009		.004	
	11th														
	12th														
	13th														
	14th														
TOTAL		36,000	12,000		48,000						12,654		9,768		

INTERPOLATION

$$\frac{654 \ \text{(Pres. Val. @ Low Rate Minus Investment)}}{2,886 \ \text{(Pres. Val. @ Low Rate Minus Pres. Val. @ High Rate)}} = .23$$

$$.23 \times \frac{15.0 \ \text{(\% High Disc. Rate Minus \% Low Disc. Rate)}}{} = 3.5$$

$$+ \ 45.0 \ \text{(\% Low Disc. Rate)}$$

$$= \ 48.5\% \ \text{ROI}$$

Project C, Without Working Capital

PROJECT EVALUATION – SINGLE INVESTMENT

INVESTMENT

Year	Annual Period	Capital Facilities	Expensed Items	Working Funds	Total Investment
	0	8,000			8,000

CASH FLOW

Year	Annual Period At End	N.A.T. Profits	Depreciation	Other	Total
	0				
	1st	4,500	2,247		6,747
	2nd	4,500	2,247		6,747
	3rd	4,500	2,247		6,747
Part Yr.	4th	2,520	1,259		3,779
	5th				
	6th				
	7th				
	8th				
	9th				
	10th				
	11th				
	12th				
	13th				
	14th				
TOTAL		16,020	8,000		24,020

CALCULATION OF RATE OF RETURN

	Trial 15% Disc. Rate		Trial 30% Disc. Rate		Trial 45% Disc. Rate		Trial 60% Disc. Rate		Trial 75% Disc. Rate	
	Factor	Present Value	Factor	Present Value	Factor	Present Value	Factor	Present Value	Factor	Present Value
	1.000		1.000		1.000		1.000		1.000	
	.870		.769		.690		.625	4,217	.571	3,853
	.756		.592		.476		.391	2,638	.327	2,206
	.658		.455		.328		.244	1,646	.187	1,262
	.572		.350		.226		.153	578	.107	404
	.497		.269		.156		.095		.061	
	.432		.207		.108		.060		.035	
	.376		.159		.074		.037		.020	
	.327		.123		.051		.023		.011	
	.284		.094		.035		.015		.006	
	.247		.073		.024		.009		.004	
								9,079		7,725

INTERPOLATION

$$\frac{1,079}{\text{(Pres. Val. @ Low Rate Minus Investment)}} \div \frac{1,354}{\text{(Pres. Val. @ Low Rate Minus Pres. Val. @ High Rate)}} = .80$$

$$.80 \times \frac{15.0}{\text{(\% High Disc. Rate Minus \% Low Disc. Rate)}}$$

$$= 12.0$$

$$+ \frac{60.0}{\text{(\% Low Disc. Rate)}}$$

$$\frac{72.0\%}{\text{ROI}}$$

127

Project A, With Working Capital

PROJECT EVALUATION – SINGLE INVESTMENT

INVESTMENT

Year	Annual Period	Capital Facilities	Expensed Items	Working Funds	Total Investment
0		10,000		10,000	20,000

CASH FLOW

					Trial 15% Disc. Rate		Trial 30% Disc. Rate		Trial 45% Disc. Rate		Trial 60% Disc. Rate		Trial 75% Disc. Rate	
Year	Annual Period At End	N.A.T. Profits	Depreciation	Other	Total	Factor	Present Value	Factor	Present Value	Factor	Present Value	Factor	Present Value	Factor	Present Value
	0					1.000		1.000		1.000		1.000		1.000	
	1st	4,375	5,000		9,375	.870	8,156	.769	7,209	.690		.625		.571	
	2nd	4,375	5,000	10,000	19,375	.756	14,648	.592	11,470	.476		.391		.327	
	3rd					.658		.455		.328		.244		.187	
	4th					.572		.350		.226		.153		.107	
	5th					.497		.269		.156		.095		.061	
	6th					.432		.207		.108		.060		.035	
	7th					.376		.159		.074		.037		.020	
	8th					.327		.123		.051		.023		.011	
	9th					.284		.094		.035		.015		.006	
	10th					.247		.073		.024		.009		.004	
	11th														
	12th														
	13th														
	14th														
TOTAL		8,750	10,000	10,000	28,750		22,804		18,679						

CALCULATION OF RATE OF RETURN

INTERPOLATION

2,804   ÷   4,125   =   .68   ×   15.0   =   10.2
(Pres. Val. @ Low Rate   (Pres. Val. @ Low Rate Minus   (% High Disc. Rate Minus
Minus Investment)   Pres. Val. @ High Rate)   % Low Disc. Rate)

+   15.0
(% Low Disc. Rate)

25.2%
ROI

Project B, With Working Capital

PROJECT EVALUATION – SINGLE INVESTMENT

INVESTMENT

Year	Annual Period	Capital Facilities	Expensed Items	Working Funds	Total Investment
	0	12,000		14,400	26,400

CASH FLOW / CALCULATION OF RATE OF RETURN

Year	Annual Period At End	N.A.T. Profits	Depreciation	Other	Total	Trial 15% Disc. Rate Factor	Present Value	Trial 30% Disc. Rate Factor	Present Value	Trial 45% Disc. Rate Factor	Present Value	Trial 60% Disc. Rate Factor	Present Value	Trial 75% Disc. Rate Factor	Present Value
	0					1.000		1.000		1.000		1.000		1.000	
	1st	4,500	1,500		6,000	.870	5,220	.769	4,614	.690		.625		.571	
	2nd	4,500	1,500		6,000	.756	4,536	.592	3,552	.476		.391		.327	
	3rd	4,500	1,500		6,000	.658	3,948	.455	2,730	.328		.244		.187	
	4th	4,500	1,500		6,000	.572	3,432	.350	2,100	.226		.153		.107	
	5th	4,500	1,500		6,000	.497	2,982	.269	1,614	.156		.095		.061	
	6th	4,500	1,500		6,000	.432	2,592	.207	1,242	.108		.060		.035	
	7th	4,500	1,500		6,000	.376	2,256	.159	954	.074		.037		.020	
	8th	4,500	1,500	14,400	20,400	.327	6,671	.123	2,509	.051		.023		.011	
	9th					.284		.094		.035		.015		.006	
	10th					.247		.073		.024		.009		.004	
	11th														
	12th														
	13th														
	14th														
TOTAL		36,000	12,000	14,400	62,400		31,637		19,315						

INTERPOLATION

$$\frac{5,237}{\text{(Pres. Val. @ Low Rate Minus Investment)}} \div \frac{12,322}{\substack{\text{(Pres. Val. @ Low Rate Minus} \\ \text{Pres. Val. @ High Rate)}}} = .43$$

$$.43 \times \frac{15.0}{\substack{\text{(% High Disc. Rate Minus} \\ \text{% Low Disc. Rate)}}} = 6.5$$

$$6.5 + \frac{15.0}{\text{(% Low Disc. Rate)}} = \frac{21.5\%}{\text{ROI}}$$

Project C, With Working Capital

PROJECT EVALUATION – SINGLE INVESTMENT

INVESTMENT

Year	Annual Period	Capital Facilities	Expensed Items	Working Funds	Total Investment
	0	8,000		14,400	22,400

CASH FLOW / CALCULATION OF RATE OF RETURN

Year	Annual Period At End	N.A.T. Profits	Depreciation	Other	Total	Trial 15% Disc. Rate Factor	Present Value	Trial 30% Disc. Rate Factor	Present Value	Trial 45% Disc. Rate Factor	Present Value	Trial 60% Disc. Rate Factor	Present Value	Trial 75% Disc. Rate Factor	Present Value
	0					1.000		1.000		1.000		1.000		1.000	
	1st	4,500	2,247		6,747	.870	5,870	.769	5,188	.690		.625		.571	
	2nd	4,500	2,247		6,747	.756	5,101	.592	3,994	.476		.391		.327	
	3rd	4,500	2,247		6,747	.658	4,440	.455	3,070	.328		.244		.187	
Part Yr.	4th	2,520	1,259	14,400	18,179	.572	10,398	.350	6,363	.226		.153		.107	
	5th					.497		.269		.156		.095		.061	
	6th					.432		.207		.108		.060		.035	
	7th					.376		.159		.074		.037		.020	
	8th					.327		.123		.051		.023		.011	
	9th					.284		.094		.035		.015		.006	
	10th					.247		.073		.024		.009		.004	
	11th														
	12th														
	13th														
	14th														
TOTAL		16,020	8,000	14,400	38,420		25,809		18,615						

INTERPOLATION

$$\frac{3,409}{\text{(Pres. Val. @ Low Rate Minus Investment)}} \div \frac{7,194}{\text{(Pres. Val. @ Low Rate Minus Pres. Val. @ High Rate)}} = .47$$

$$\times \frac{15.0}{\text{(\% High Disc. Rate Minus \% Low Disc. Rate)}} = 7.1$$

$$+ \frac{15.0}{\text{(\% Low Disc. Rate)}}$$

$$\frac{22.1\%}{\text{ROI}}$$

130

ROI for the Business

Investment:

1. Current assets _____
2. Less: Current liabilities _____
3. Net working capital _____
4. Plus: Investments in subsidiaries _____
5.   Net goodwill, patents, etc. _____
6.   Land _____
7.   Other nonwasting assets _____
8. Total nonwasting assets _____

9. Net fixed assets _____
10. Plus: Reserve for depreciation _____
11. Gross fixed assets _____
12. Total investment in business _____

Cash flow:

13. After-tax profits _____
14. Depreciation _____
15. Inc./(Dec.) in deferred taxes (If tax depreciation different from Line 14.) _____
16. After-tax interest on long-term debt _____
17. Subtotal _____
18. Less: Any cash flow resulting from amortization of assets on Line 5 _____
19. Total cash flow _____

20. Average asset life _____
21. ROI for the business _____

Stock Valuation

22. Total investment in business (Line 12) _____
23. Less: Long-term debt _____
24.   Preferred stock _____
25. Investment applicable to common shareholders _____

26. Total cash flow (Line 19) _____
27. Less: Preferred stock dividend _____
  After-tax interest on long-term debt (Line 16) _____
29. Cash flow applicable to common shareholders _____
30. ROI on investment applicable to common shareholders _____
31. No. of common shares _____

Normal Stock Value Calculation Based on 10% ROI:

$$(\underline{\quad\quad\quad} \div \underline{\quad.10\quad}) \times (\underline{\quad\quad\quad} \div \underline{\quad\quad\quad}) = \underline{\quad\quad\quad}$$

  (Line 30) (Desired   (Line 25) (Line 31)   (Normal
        ROI)   Stock Value)

NOTE: The above excludes treatment of capitalized leases. (See Chapter 10.)

Appendix E (to Chapter 9): Discussion of Reinvestment of Cash Flow from Depreciable Assets

One of the principal difficulties in penetrating ROI mathematics for the perpetuation of Company B in Chart 9-1 arises because conventional bookkeeping doesn't parallel the true ROI concept. Specifically, five-year depreciation (principal reduction) of the $1,000 asset is taken in uniform $200 bites. But "paying off the mortgage" doesn't work that way. Instead, at a 10% ROI, the first year's cash flow of $264 is applied as follows: $100 (i.e., 10%) to interest and the balance of $164 to a reduction of the principal. Everything comes out even at the end of five years, but the inner workings are different.

In addition, the absolute dollar return associated with a 10% ROI for Company B is not of itself directly comparable with that for Company A. This is because A always has $1,000 put out to work, whereas the balance for B is gradually declining. In other words, Company B's ROI is, by definition, the return on that portion of the investment outstanding for as long as it is outstanding. The ROI is in fact 10%, but because the investment base for B is declining, the total dollar results over the five years also will be less. Specifically, for its $1,000 initial outlay Company A will collect $100 a year for five years and will also recoup the $1,000 invested initially—a total of $1,500. On the other hand, for its $1,000 outlay Company B will collect $264 × 5, or $1,320, over the five-year period, a smaller amount simply because B's investment base was declining during the period. To repeat, the ROI percentage is the same—just the dollar return is lower because B's absolute investment also was lower during the five years being measured.

When the objective is to maintain comparability between A and B in absolute dollars, B then has the obligation to maintain a constant investment base of $1,000. To do this, a certain amount of its cash flow must be put back to work. One cannot use the full $200 shown as depreciation for this purpose, since that would exceed the constant amount invested by A. In other words, the return of principal included in B's $264 first-year cash flow is $164, and therefore only this amount can be put back to bring B up to a "fully invested" position of $1,000. It is here that a reconciliation between mathematics and bookkeeping becomes quite complex—and beyond the limits researched by the author. Consequently, the alternative is to revert temporarily to a philosophical approach and take refuge behind the basic underlying assumption regarding B—which is correct—that the ROI shown is accurate and proper for the condition portrayed, i.e., "paying off the mortgage." It isn't the math that causes trouble, it's the fact that conventional bookkeeping does not always parallel the realities of ROI.

Consolation comes from the fact that it is not essential to thoroughly understand and resolve this particular matter. It's an esoteric—and largely incidental—detail. The ROI concept and applications contained in this book are not at all harmed or degraded by this bit of unfinished business.

Index